Kabbalah of Prayer

02/2020

To Michael,

In memory of Eileen,
whose sound evoked
grace, beauty, and
delight,

As always,
Roland

Also by Shulamit Elson

Books
*Brooklyn Bodhisattvas, A Book of Visions and
Kabballistic Poetry*
(ISBN # 1-929630-02-6)

Audio CDs
Beyond Words: The Sounds of the Kabballah
Compact Disc (ISBN # 1-929630-03-4)

*Vibration: Shulamit and the Drepung Gomang
Buddhist Monks*
Compact Disc (ISBN # 1-929630-04-02)

Kabbalah of Prayer
Sacred Sounds and the Soul's Journey

Shulamit Elson

Published by Lindisfarne Books
400 Main Street
Great Barrington, MA 01230
www. lindisfarne.org

Printed in the United States of America.

Library of Congress Cataloging-in-Publication Data

Shulamit.
Kabbalah of prayer : sacred sounds and the soul's journey/
by Shulamit Elson.
p. cm.
ISBN 1-58420-017-0—ISBN 1-58420-017-0
1. Cabala. 2. Prayer—Judaism. 3. Sound—Religious
aspects—Judaism. I. Title.
BM525.S635 2004
96.7'12—dc22
2003027288

FOR MY FATHER AND MOTHER
NATHAN AND JOSEPHINE LEVINE

AND

MY HUSBAND AND PARTNER
CHAD STEPHEN ELSON

"You are not expected to complete the work, nor are you permitted to abandon it."

Rabbi Tarfon
Pirke Avot

Acknowledgements

THIS BOOK IS BASED on sacred Jewish texts, including the received tradition and wisdom of the *Kabbalah*, as well as the teachings of blessed Rabbis, mystics, and sages of past generations.

The use of sacred sounds was taught to me by my revered teacher, who transmitted them to me over a period of years. His wisdom and teaching fell on fertile ground owing to my parents, Josephine and Nathan Levine, who provided me with an education in *Torah* and Hebrew studies.

In addition, many wonderful individuals have helped to make this book possible:

My husband and life partner, Chad Stephen Elson, whose unflagging support, abiding love, critical intelligence, and humor informed every stage of this process.

Christopher Bamford of SteinerBooks/Lindisfarne Books, who gave invaluable guidance in birthing this book.

William Arnone, Judy Atwood, Deborah Barkow, Rabbi Eliyahu Bergstein, Rose and Joe Esposito, Rabbi Joshua Grater, Dr. Yitzhak Hayutman, Ph.D., Betty Jackson, Jenny Krouse, Debbie Lawrence, and Hadass Melamed, who gave generously and lovingly of their time and wisdom. Their input strengthened this book.

Sincere appreciation goes to Mary Giddens, of SteinerBooks, for gracious support in layout and design, to Beth Robbins for editorial comments, to Curran Giddens for illustrations, and to Nicky Heron and Sarah Gallogly for their invaluable editorial assistance.

Special thanks to Harold Akrongold and Richard Smoley for helping to find this book a home.

And finally, thanks are due all my students who shared their thoughts with me as this book unfolded.

Perfection is an attribute of God alone. I assume full responsibility for any errors or misjudgements that this book may contain.

A Gift for the Reader

❦

Hebrew is a sacred language. The sound of particular Hebrew letters, animated by sacred vowel sounds, produces vibrations that can have a profound spiritual effect.

I have prepared a special place for you to listen as I pronounce many of the Hebrew words in this book. You will also be able to hear my voice as I share with you the vowel sounds used in the Sound Prayers found in the last chapter.

Please visit:

www.KabbalahofPrayer.com/sacredsounds

There you will find audio files that you can listen to as often as you like.

Note on Pronouns

When writing about God, an author must invariably make decisions about the use of the personal pronouns "He," "She," and "It."

The Creator has both male and female aspects but no gender. For the sake of readability, I have chosen to use the pronoun "He" when using words such as "God" and "The Holy One."

I have chosen to use the word "She" when referring to the *Shekhinah*, which is the female aspect of God's presence on earth, and "It" when using the term *Ein Sof* or Limitless One.

Note on Transliteration, Pronunciation, and Definitions

Many Hebrew words and names have more than one accepted transliteration into English. I have chosen to use those transliterations which I feel come closest to correct pronunciations. A separate guide to the pronunciation and definition of Hebrew words and names occurring in the text can be found in the Appendices.

Note on Translations

All translations from Hebrew and Aramaic texts into English are my own unless otherwise indicated. I am grateful to Dr. Yitzhak Hayutman, Ph.D., and Hadass Melamed, who assisted me in these translations.

When translating the writings commonly referred to as the *Zohar*, I have, at times, found the Soncino Press English translation useful. In such cases, I have referred to my source as the *Zohar*. In all other instances, I cite as my original source the *Sefer haZohar*.

Contents

Foreword

SHULAMIT ELSON HAS CRAFTED a personal and practical introduction to a subject that many readers in the past have found arcane and impenetrable. Writers on mysticism often obscure what they claim to illuminate, burdening their prose with unfamiliar language. Shulamit will have none of that; she explains everything she says in a way that facilitates understanding and practice.

In the *Kabbalah*, other worlds convey the significance behind any time and place we might live in. Shulamit gently insists on this mystical conception of reality as she narrates how she arrived at an experience and an understanding that made the *Kabbalah* the center of her own devotion. She writes with the love of a dedicated practitioner, but also with historical awareness. In the study of the *Kabbalah* at any level, that is crucial.

From the earliest sources of the Bible, visions of God enthroned in his heavenly court have shaped the faith of Israel. The prophet Ezekiel gave the awareness of divine presence the name of the chariot, the *Merkavah* that could disclose itself everywhere, conveying its power wherever a receptive seer might be found.

Practitioners of divine presence embraced these traditions. The verb *kabal* means to grasp or hold fast, and *kabballah* refers to a precious tradition one embraces from a master with all one's strength. Shulamit specializes in the form of this embrace that emerged fully during the Middle Ages, especially in the enriching mix of Judaic, Muslim, and neo-Platonic cultures in Spain and the south of France during the thirteenth century of the Common Era.

By this time two foci of meditation were prevalent. One was on the *shiur komah*, the "measure of the body." This referred to God's corporal reality, of which the human body—in the divine image and likeness— provided a reflection. The other focus involved discerning the *Sefirot*, the emanations that vibrated outward from God and made all that is, and resonated with the formations of the body. The *Kabbalah* at this stage represented the highest accomplishment of Judaic mysticism as a philosophical and personal discipline.

Conventional scholarship has long sidelined the *Kabbalah*; even worse, commercial exploitation has trivialized its subtle teaching. But no mystical tradition better explores the intersecting mysteries of human character and divine presence than the medieval *Kabbalah*, and no writer offers a better primer in its contemporary practice and understanding than Shulamit Elson.

Bruce Chilton
Executive Director, Institute of Advanced Theology
Bernard Iddings Bell Professor of Religion
Bard College

ℐntroduction

BURIED WITHIN THE SOUL of every human being lies
a sacred spark. This spark manifests as our drive to
grow and develop spiritually—a drive arising from the
core of our being. The ground of this driving force lies
in the memory of our original state of oneness with
God. Deep within the soul of each of us is the knowledge that before birth we were united with the Holy
One and that, despite the appearance of duality and
separation here on earth, this state of oneness is our
birthright.

Most of us first experience our spiritual drive as a
deep yearning, a gnawing sense of incompleteness, a
recognition that something we cannot name is missing
from our lives. This yearning can continue unabated for
years while we busily occupy ourselves with the rewards

and sorrows of the everyday. The result is a deep subterranean sadness.

The intensity of spiritual yearning varies from person to person, yet all know something of its pull. My own story follows a trajectory from an ordinary existence, filled with dissatisfaction and longing, to a life of fulfillment and spiritual connection. Through many upheavals, great confusion, and much searching, I was led inexorably toward a higher state of awareness. I have come to see how the development of individual consciousness mirrors the development of the consciousness of the universe, and how when we refuse to change and grow, change is forced upon us.

At this time on earth, something new is attempting to be born; a higher consciousness is struggling to emerge. This consciousness, and the force behind it, is coming from the upper World of Creation. In the *Kabbalah*, the mystical tradition within Judaism, this world is called *Olam haBeriah*.

It is a consciousness that has the potential to uplift and transform, sweeping away our traditional concepts of duality, division, and separation, in a great spiritual awakening. In this birthing process there are both positive and negative forces at work and there is obvious destruction. The coming times, however, need not bring unending suffering or relentless violence.

It is a central teaching of *Kabbalah* that, in addition to influencing our physical world, every soul has the ability to influence the spiritual worlds above. These worlds play an important role in determining unfolding events on earth. Thus, each one of us can affect the future in ways far beyond what we ordinarily think possible. This is a gift that brings extraordinary opportunity as well as great responsibility. The forces being unleashed upon our planet are beyond the control of any institution, state, or government, and it is now up to each of us to direct the future.

Despite recent events, rest assured that within the chaos swirling around us, a pattern is emerging, no matter how undetectable it might be at this moment. Therefore, it is of the utmost importance that each one of us hold fast to love, act honorably with compassion and courage, and direct our thoughts, prayers, and actions toward the shaping of a positive future.

From a mystical standpoint, the teaching is "as above, so below." The upper spiritual worlds are as real as our own, and all the worlds are connected. What we do here affects the upper worlds, and what happens above helps determine our fate here.

By incorporating the wisdom of the *Kabbalah* into our lives, we can raise our spiritual consciousness to sustain our families and ourselves through whatever the future holds. Using the Kabbalistic practice of Sound Prayer, we can raise our voices, stir our hearts, and send sacred vibrations through all the upper worlds, helping to align them, bringing angelic help and spiritual support. In so doing, we can each personally make a difference as we contribute to *Tikkun Olam*, the repair of the world.

Shulamit Elson
High Falls, New York
January 2004

Part One

1

The Path of Kabbalah

IT IS WRITTEN THAT God cast Adam and Eve out of the Garden of Eden for disobeying Him by eating from the Tree of Knowledge of Good and Evil. Then, to prevent them from eating of the Tree of Eternal Life, God placed angels and a revolving flaming sword in front of the tree to block the way.[1]

For one who is prepared and worthy, however, the angels guarding the Tree of Life step aside, and the sword averts its blade. With God's blessing, such an individual can journey past the angels and the flaming sword to taste of the Tree of Life's fruit and live joyously in the Divine Presence.

In every generation, there are men and women who seek to make this journey using *Kabbalah*, the ancient Jewish mystical path. By striving to unlock the mysteries of the universe and to align with the forces of creation, students of *Kabbalah* attempt to make their way back to God.

One of the most important teachings of *Kabbalah* is that in addition to our *nefesh*, or animal soul, which we share with all living creatures, each human being possesses a *neshamah*, or higher soul. Our higher soul can never be debased or corrupted and it knows everything we need to know about the universe and our place within it. It is a part of us literally touched by God, and it offers each of us the possibility of direct contact with the angelic world and the forces of creation.

The *Kabbalah* teaches that while each of us has a higher soul as a gift from the Creator, almost all of us begin life with it hidden and dormant, in need of awakening. Most of us spend our lives with an underlying sense that a part of ourselves is missing. The part of us that we experience as missing is our *neshamah*, our higher soul, longing to be awakened. Spiritual growth is a process of awakening our higher soul, becoming worthy to approach the Tree of Life, taste of its fruit, and reside joyously in the Garden of Eden.

As we strive to awaken our higher soul, it is important to make a distinction between the symbolism of The Tree of Knowledge of Good and Evil and The Tree of Life. The Tree of Knowledge represents our basic understanding of right and wrong. Regardless of how we actually behave, all of us possess this knowledge simply by virtue of being human. The Tree of Life, on the other hand, offers a treasure that each of us must individually work to achieve.

The awakening of our higher soul results in remembering our reason for being, our place in the universe and our relationship to God. In the irrefutable knowledge that it brings, we are welcomed back into the unifying embrace of the Eternal. In this awakening, we find a spiritual and physical wholeness capable of replacing the roller coaster of everyday human emotions with the deep and abiding joy that is our birthright. It is this return we each seek throughout life.

The *Kabbalah* offers a path to the awakening of our higher soul based on an understanding of how our thoughts, speech, and actions either elevate or degrade our nature. On this path, the *Kabbalah* teaches us the power of prayer by deepening our understanding of the true nature of prayer and its effect on ourselves and the upper worlds. Through the study of *Kabbalah*, we come to understand that by strengthening our connection to the upper worlds through the act of prayer, we align our own spiritual essence, our own vibration, with the vibration of the Eternal.

The path of spiritual awakening is not an easy one. When we seek a personal relationship with God, we set out alone, almost always unsure of reaching our goal and often unconvinced as to the wisdom of pursuing it.

In large part, this is because we are constantly taught that the everyday ideas of success—an attractive body, large sums of money, increased life expectancy, and a reasonably successful career and family life—are all there is and all that we have a right to expect. We are led to believe that if there is a God, He is far removed from our day-to-day concerns—seemingly more involved with us after we die than while we are alive.

There comes a time in each of our lives, however, when we know this worldview to be false. Then, with all our doubts, fears and flaws, we cry out, yearning for something more. Some years ago, just such a deep yearning led me to embark on my own spiritual journey. This meant leaving the rewards and security of a traditional career for the uncertainty of the mystic's path. This is where my own story begins.

Shulamit, the name given to me at birth, comes from King Solomon's *Shir Hashirim* or Song of Songs, a biblical love poem of great beauty and mystical significance. It was a big name for a small child, unpronounceable to many and often a cause of embarrassment. It set me apart at an early age, and it would be many years before I would grow into it.

The story of that growth is the description of my soul's journey. It is a journey from separation, anxiety, and confusion, into a state of deepening integration, faith, and clarity. It is a journey from an ordinary life filled with restlessness and sorrow, to a mystical path of awakening that led to God, not as an abstraction but as a living Presence.

During my first 40 years, I led two distinctly separate lives, serving two masters, neither with a full heart. My inner life and my outer life had little relationship to each other and I had no clue as to how to live either of them successfully, let alone as a whole human being. Throughout this time, I lived uncomfortably in my skin, constantly trying to shove the square peg of myself into the round hole of a world based on beliefs I knew to be shallow, false, and misguided, but could neither refute or replace.

In my later years, I have come to live my own truth with the knowledge that I am finally embodying my soul's purpose. I have moved from being a frightened slave to a devoted servant, ultimately accepting the responsibility of my work as a messenger and spiritual teacher.

Looking back, where confusion and unhappiness reigned, I now see the seeds of my own spiritual development. In errors and mistaken judgements, and the suffering they brought, I recognize signposts that eventually led me to my true path. In the spiritual teachings of the *Kabbalah*, I have found the answer to questions that have been with me for as long as I can remember.

My early childhood, viewed from the outside, gave very little indication of the extraordinary mystical journey I would eventually embark upon. Raised in an Orthodox Jewish family, I attended a religious school, or *Yeshivah*, from first grade through high school. There I received a thorough education in both secular and Jewish studies. I was fluent in both English and

Hebrew and was thought of as attractive, intelligent, and well adjusted. I was expected to marry well, have lots of children, and lead a traditional observant religious life.

These outward appearances, however, were quite deceiving. From early on, my inner life was in constant turmoil. To this day, I have the vivid memory of being not quite three years old, standing lower than the dining room table, looking up at my parents and brothers, and asking myself, "Who are these people?" I had no answer except the certain knowledge that I did not belong among them.

Throughout childhood, my family's daily concerns were not my concerns, and their religious practices seemed irrelevant to my life. Rarely at ease, I continually felt that I was supposed to be somewhere else, but had no idea where that could be.

As I grew up, neither my classmates at school nor the adults around me were a significant part of my life. Instead, I became a voracious reader and lived almost exclusively in my private thoughts. In the characters of the books I read, I searched for a familiar face, trying over and over to imagine where I belonged. In the end, since neither my books nor my imagination held the key, I viewed my childhood as a prison from which time alone could deliver me. The release I yearned for was still many years away.

At seventeen, using marriage as a way out, I finally left home. I divorced shortly thereafter, feeling free for the first time in my life. Abandoning Orthodox Judaism, I enrolled at New York University, moved to Manhattan, and completely immersed myself in the outside world. My college years, however, provided more of a distraction from my struggles than answers to my burning questions. In fact, these questions slowly and quietly faded into the background. The reality was that I was not ready for the answers.

After graduation, I fell in love with an artist and moved with him to Paris, becoming part of the lively expatriate scene. I traveled throughout France and then to Spain and Morocco, and began to write poetry. But I soon lost my footing. The rootless bohemian life lost its charm, my romance crashed, my writing was leading nowhere, and I was certainly no closer to finding what I was looking for.

Finally, with a profound sense of loss, I returned to New York. Once again, my deep-seated belief that there was a particular reason for my being here, some place I belonged, and something I needed to do, took center stage. I was without a clue, however, where to turn next and quickly fell into despair.

It was not long before I became very ill. For no apparent reason both my kidneys began to fail. After many tests and a painful biopsy, my doctor reluctantly told me that he had never seen anyone with my condition recover.

It was also during this period, that I watched my family's business fail, my parents lose their home, and my father lose his self-esteem. In his last sad years, stripped of his bulwark of material security against the vicissitudes of the world, he struggled to rebuild his life and regain his dignity. He died of a heart attack before accomplishing either.

Meanwhile, I met a man who wanted to marry me despite my illness. I accepted his proposal and we became engaged. My father died on the same day that I was to introduce him to my fiancé. I was unable to reach my fiancé to tell of my father's death, and he arrived at my parent's home in a beautiful cream-colored suit with a box of chocolates in his hand. He was ushered into a house of mourning. It seemed to me on that day, my entire world was one of sorrow and loss.

Immediately after my marriage, I began a highly experimental course of treatment that involved taking massive doses of cortisone. Very quickly every part of me, inside and out, was affected by the drug. My entire body was in pain and I felt afflicted with the trials of Job. The drug caused my face to change completely, growing round and breaking out with acne. My appearance was so altered that even my best friends did not recognize me. I actually found myself questioning my own identity—for who was I if not my face?

As my condition worsened, and it became clear that the cortisone was not working, my doctor and I agreed to stop all treatment. I was sent home with kind words to the effect that I should just accept my fate and try to live as comfortably as possible. Dialysis would be of some help, but I was assured of rapidly declining health and a greatly foreshortened life lived in cold and heartless hospital corridors.

Ironically, I was beginning one of the happiest periods of my life thus far. At twenty-six, confronted by an incurable illness and my own mortality, I began to surrender to each day as it came; the ensuing peace and calm prompted me to spend a good deal of time pondering the nature of happiness itself. This was another question, however, whose answer would come much later in my life.

Then, many months later and just like that, my illness suddenly and completely disappeared, as simply and quickly as it arrived. It took my doctor quite some time to accept my newfound state of health. In the end he was reduced to simply shaking his head and calling it an unexplained and mysterious "spontaneous remission."

I, on the other hand, called it a miracle. For some time I was acutely conscious of my vital force—in its simplicity and power. I could actually feel my life's blood coursing through my veins and, while it was some time before I could integrate the lessons of this period, I have never forgotten that feeling.

After my recovery I set out to build a life devoted to the pursuit of financial security. While my inner yearning for meaning and connection never totally left me, it was almost completely set aside in favor of seeking the everyday rewards of the material world.

Looking back on this period, I now understand that my desire for a respected and lucrative career was a confused way of trying to fit in. Restored to health, I simply decided to accept reality as described to me and find fulfillment in what seemed to work for everyone else.

In the years that followed, I struggled hard to achieve the "good life." I worked for several large corporations and ended up with all the trappings of traditional success: a large house in an upscale suburb, a manicured lawn, a nice car, and the clothes to match. In addition, I was blessed with a beautiful young daughter. The fact that I was terribly unhappy was my only difficulty.

The ensuing years were ones of continual confusion and inner conflict. I wandered in a hall of mirrors— everywhere I looked I saw the reflections of my own ambivalence and loss. Then, after fifteen years of gradually drifting apart, my husband and I divorced. The day we separated, all the people I knew socially stopped talking to me. At this significant break in my life, as the old structures fell away, and before new ones took their place, a richness arose out of my own nature. I was flooded with memories of my childhood struggles. All of a sudden, the certain knowledge that some piece of me was missing returned, along with the understanding that I would never be truly happy until I reconnected with it. My yearning for something more now became impossible to set aside.

At the same time, my business career was doing better than ever. Months before my divorce, I had started my own management consulting firm and projects from large and small companies were starting to pour in. These were commitments I could not ignore, but at the same time, I was adamant about finding a way to re-dedicate myself to my inner life. I did not have long to wait.

My journey started with waking visions that could not be denied. The first was a large, beautiful bird standing silently in the doorway of my bedroom—full of mystery and potential. Then began a series of startlingly vivid experiences of angels and messengers from other realms. Sometimes they came in human form, sometimes simply as animated lights that filled me with joy. These entities seemed to belong to a hierarchy, each one sent to show me a different aspect of worlds whose rules and rewards were strikingly different from the world I knew. I now understand that their role was to grab hold of my being, so that nothing would be more important than to follow where they led. In this they succeeded.

Not long after my visions began, I was visited by a spirit who came to me in the form of a Native American. In his presence, I felt ineffable love and a deep peace, yet at the same time great sadness. Part of me longed to stay with him forever, but I quickly became overwhelmed and turned away. When I looked back, much to my sorrow, he had disappeared. This pattern was repeated again and again. Each time a vision took hold, I longed for it to stay, but I was clearly not in control. My visions seemed to come and go as they pleased.

To stay in contact with the beings that were visiting me, I began to meditate for long periods. After each vision I would close my eyes and spend hours focused on a single image from the vision left over in my mind's eye. As the months went by, I slowly began to develop gifts that I could not explain. Often, I "saw" things before they happened, many other times I found that I knew things about people's struggles without their having to tell me.

Excited, awestruck, and sometimes terrified, I struggled down this new path, feeling more and more removed from the everyday world around me. While I continued to have many "normal" days, there were increasing periods when I completely lost any sense of the importance of the outside world, and nothing seemed to matter except my visions. At times, I became overly sensitive, like a snake that had shed its skin without having a new one to replace it. I often had difficulty keeping track of time, and feared for my well-being and my sanity. Fortunately, I met a soul mate during this time, a man who encouraged me to be open to my strange and extraordinary experiences. His love helped to keep me grounded and gave me great support.

Then, suddenly, I was offered a chance to return to "reality" with a vengeance. Despite the fact that my inner life and my visions were leading me elsewhere, my consulting firm had continued to flourish and now one of my clients, a Wall Street investment bank, offered me a full time position. Although this would mean working long hours in a competitive environment, I accepted the offer, thinking of it as an opportunity to take a break from my intense visionary experiences. I would soon discover just how impossible that had become.

As I began work at my new job, my visions became increasingly intense. I did, however, manage to function efficiently in between their visits. I continued this way for several years—my visions and gifts a secret from those around me. These were difficult times, as I was strung between two worlds—the one I did not belong to and the promised land that I longed to inhabit.

Then one night I was awakened by another huge bird appearing at the foot of my bed. It was pure white with thin pulsing veins underneath its skin that cast a light blue shadow. There was a ruby in its head and its back had the shiny richness of patent leather. The outline of its feathers was cut very deep, reminding me of the dry, cracked earth of the desert in the Southwest before the rains come. Its only communication to me was that I should not touch its back.

The bird accompanied me to work at the investment bank and its presence was a great joy, producing feelings of deep love. It was an experience so rich and intense that it could not be sustained for more than a few moments at a time before I had to turn away. The bird stayed close by me for a week and then it was gone. For several days afterward, when I looked to the sky, I could see it flying, joined by others of its kind, and then that vision too disappeared.

But by then the call was clear. Within days I made a decision to leave my work on Wall Street and begin a full-time search for answers and an explanation of my gifts and visions. My soul mate, whom I had recently married, encouraged my resolve and I soon left the everyday world of work and career completely behind.

With no extraneous activities to divert my gaze, I began a serious quest. I pored over countless spiritual books and met with teachers and gurus from many different traditions. I attended numerous lectures and presentations by thoughtful thinkers and charismatic speakers. Nothing resonated, nothing touched my heart. Although my longing for guidance continued, even my visions began to subside.

At the end of a particularly difficult period, I went to Jamaica for a holiday. Inexplicably, I became quite sensitive to the sun and spent most of my days indoors. I would only emerge at dusk to stare at the sea beyond the terrace of my room.

One evening, as I gazed out to sea, I saw myself floating beyond the waves, my head bobbing in the water. Suddenly I had the clear knowledge that something important was about to happen. Moments later, I became overwhelmed by a presence, different from anything I had experienced before. He was a teacher that, I would later discover, the *Kabbalah* refers to as an "answering angel." He was a being without form, yet he touched me as tenderly, as completely, and as intimately as a lover. His message, conveyed in silence, was that everything that had happened to me in my past had happened for a reason. This simple statement reached into the core of my being. I have never viewed the world in the same way.

After I returned home, my answering angel began to instruct me in the making of certain sounds with my voice. No explanation was given, just instruction. Lacking a physical body, he communicated directly, without the intermediary of speech, yet his teachings were as real and commanding as those of any human teacher.

I had no rational reason for following his directions, nor did I have any idea what purpose could be served by the sounds I was being taught. I had no particular ability to carry a tune, nor did I have a talent for chanting. Such was my trust, however, that I continued practicing day after day. As our sessions continued, I learned to live in a state of unknowing and to allow myself to work at something simply because it felt right, without having a specific goal. Both were lessons that would prove invaluable in the years to follow.

Then one night, as I lay in bed chanting my sounds, I felt an unintelligible whispering in my ear. Closing my eyes, I was propelled into another space. I was a star in the heavens, suspended in the cosmos, one of billions and billions of stars, each with its own consciousness and yet each part of a universal consciousness to which

I too belonged. It was a sublime experience with none of the obtuse symbolism or emotional baggage of a dream. It was palpable and real, an event of total clarity.

I am describing this event in the first person, but during the actual experience there was, in fact, no sense of self: my "I" was absent. Then, at a certain point, an awareness of this absence arose and immediately a fear of death took hold. In an instant I was back in my normal state of consciousness. Lying in my bed, with my heart beating strong in my chest, I spoke aloud the words: "I have lost everything that I have ever known." At the time, I had no idea why I said this.

Closing my eyes once again, the exact same experience unfolded. There was the complete absence of self and the participation in an individual as well as universal consciousness, then a sudden realization of being "absent," followed by an abrupt return to normal consciousness.

Over the course of the next several weeks, I slowly came to understand that I had been given a great gift; I had experienced the multidimensional, limitlessness nature of consciousness. I realized that I had returned to the time before birth, before incarnation, before my soul descended to earth. I also realized that, in a real sense, I was still there.

As the months passed, my answering angel remained close by my side, helping me assimilate my latest vision. This required intense work as he guided me in the use of the sounds I had been taught, enabling me to access many new levels of understanding within myself. Then, after more than a year of such work, my teacher directed me to seek in the writings of the *Kabbalah* for further guidance.

Initially, I was extremely reluctant to delve into *Kabbalah*. I remembered the religious prohibitions surrounding it, including the restrictions against women studying any of its writings. But in the end, the drive to continue my study and the thirst for answers and a further explanation of my visionary experiences overcame any fears. With my teacher's reassurance, I set out to become a serious student of *Kabbalah*.

The *Kabbalah* traces its beginnings to the time of the biblical patriarch Abraham. In both written and oral form, its wisdom has been carefully handed down from master to student, capturing the imagination of religious scholars and spiritual seekers for thousands of years. In addition, while often unrecognized, many Kabbalistic ideas permeate the Jewish prayer book, or *Siddur*, and remain part of accepted liturgy to the present day.

The books that make up the foundation writings of *Kabbalah* include the *Sefer Yetzirah*, or The Book of Creation, whose first date of appearance in written form is unknown, but whose oral teachings date back before the first century, *Sefer haBahir*, or The Book of Illumination, first published in the late twelfth century, and *Sefer haZohar*, known as The Book of Splendor, first printed in the late thirteenth century.[2]

These books are part of a vital tradition, kept alive over the centuries by dedicated spiritual seekers committed to finding answers to questions about the nature of creation, the Creator, and our place within the divinely ordered universe. Their goal is to uncover a mystical path to oneness with God through study of the hidden esoteric meaning of the *Tanakh*, the Hebrew Holy Scriptures.

In the Middle Ages, a significant amount of the unpublished oral *Kabbalah* tradition was written down in great seats of spiritual learning such as Gerona in Spain and Provence in France. One result was that access to the *Kabbalah*'s mystical teachings slowly expanded beyond a relatively small circle of Kabbalist Rabbis and scholars.

Then, towards the end of the seventeenth century, access to the *Kabbalah*'s teachings once again became increasingly limited. Its teachings were hidden away, in part, because of their misuse by a false Messiah named Sabbatai Tzvi in the mid-sixteen hundreds.

Invoking the writings of the *Kabbalah*, Sabbatai declared himself the long-awaited savior of the Jewish people and succeeded in gathering thousands of fervent followers in Jewish communities throughout Europe, the Ottoman Empire, and the Holy Land. With the assistance of a "prophet" named Nathan of Gaza, and a considerable number of learned *Kabbalah* scholars and respected Rabbis, Sabbatai's influence extended to almost every Jewish community in the world.[3]

When Sabbatai converted to Islam, rather than be put to death by the Sultan of Turkey, it became clear that he was not, in fact, the Messiah. This realization, which resulted in intense sorrow and tribulation among the Jews of the world, prompted the religious leaders of the day to reevaluate the place of *Kabbalah* within Judaism. Eventually, the wisdom of allowing open access to the *Kabbalah* was seriously questioned, and a number of restrictions were put in place in an attempt to limit its study to those who were sufficiently mature, both emotionally and spiritually.

Despite these restrictions, a great deal of misinterpretation and misunderstanding continues to surround Kabbalistic teaching. Much of this misunderstanding results from the fact that significant parts of the *Kabbalah* are devoted to the task of penetrating the mysteries of Hebrew Holy Scripture by unraveling intricate relationships and hidden sacred meanings in its individual Hebrew letters, words, and phrases. This is extremely difficult material.

In addition, it is no accident that the word *kabbalah* has the same root as the Hebrew word *hakbalah* which means "parallels," since much of the *Kabbalah* focuses on establishing parallels between things that, on the surface, appear to be unrelated. This is often done through laborious examination of intricate correlations between individual words, phrases and stories found in Hebrew Holy Scripture.

The Kabbalist's search for parallels also makes

extensive use of the fact that the Hebrew language consists of two distinct elements, the twenty-two letters of
the alphabet as well as various sets of markings above,
below, and within the letters. These markings, called
nekudot, or vowel points, add specific vowel sounds to
the pronunciation of Hebrew words. Thus, the letters
of two Hebrew words can be identical, while their pronunciation and meaning will differ as a result of having
different vowel points. Between such words, the
Kabbalist will often find and explore relationships,
which lead to conclusions that require careful study.

For example, while the Hebrew words for "blessing" and for "a fresh pool of water" have different
vowel points and are pronounced differently, they are
both spelled with exactly the same letters, ברכה. The
relationship between these two words is both obvious
and complex.

Additionally, by using the numeric values traditionally assigned to each of the letters of the Hebrew alphabet, many Kabbalists seek to find mystical connections
based on the numerical equivalence of different words
and phrases in Hebrew Holy Scripture. This practice,
called *gematria*, demands extensive knowledge of the
Hebrew language, and its conclusions need to be
explored with great care.

Just as demanding are the *Kabbalah*'s intricate commentaries, which seek to explain the hidden meaning
buried deep within the pages of various holy writings.
These commentaries are often obscure and can seem

quite impenetrable. In large part, this is because the *Kabbalah* is a mystic's path to God, sharing insights into a world that is essentially non-conceptual and non-dual. This world does not easily lend itself to straightforward explication. Indeed, much of the power of the written *Kabbalah* lies in its highly poetic language, requiring us to look beyond a literal reading in order to extract its wisdom.

Also contributing to a lack of understanding of *Kabbalah* is the fact that many books and scholarly treatises that give critical insight into the *Kabbalah*'s teachings have yet to be translated from the original ancient Hebrew and Aramaic. These include works by such towering figures in the world of *Kabbalah* as the sixteenth century Rabbi, Isaac Luria, and the great mystical thinkers of the thirteenth century, Rabbi Joseph Gikatila and Rabbi Abraham Abulafia.

The fact that the *Kabbalah* is extremely difficult to comprehend, and easily misunderstood, is far from academic. As the *Kabbalah* becomes more widely available, it is critical for readers to understand that the power of its teachings and meditative practices is so great that those who study it without guidance can actually come to harm.

On the other hand, the *Kabbalah* offers great gifts to those who approach it with the requisite respect and the guidance of a knowledgeable teacher. It is worth noting, in this regard, that the Hebrew word *kabbalah* actually means "receiving," and that throughout history, the ancient wisdom of *Kabbalah* has been received by individuals through an intimate relationship with a *maggid* or teacher, one who carefully guides the student on the path to the hidden. In this way, and in each generation, the *Kabbalah*'s teachings are renewed as sincere seekers of truth, longing to experience the living God for themselves, strive alongside their teachers to open their hearts to receive its wisdom.

Most important, the study of *Kabbalah* demands a righteous heart and pure intention. Those who seek its mysteries to learn how to manipulate the world to their personal advantage are embarked on a dangerous path, and those who use its teachings to seek power over others will find themselves drawn to darkness.

It is only by seeking God's embrace, rather than undeserved wealth or individual power, that students of *Kabbalah* can carve a protected path for themselves. It is only our own deep personal yearning after the Holy One that secures the protection of the forces of the angelic world and the messengers of God to help and guide us.

This is why in the Hebrew Bible, or *Torah*, also known as the Five Books of Moses, the Creator is referred to as "the God of Abraham, the God of Isaac, and the God of Jacob"[4] rather than the God of Abraham, Isaac, and Jacob. The specific wording of this biblical phrase points to the fact that every one of us must individually find God for ourselves, as did each of these three spiritual seekers.

As my own study of the *Kabbalah* continued with my teacher over the years, I found an extraordinarily rich tradition and a universal guide for spiritual awakening. Its universality resides in the fact that while there are many different paths to enlightenment, and many names for the Holy One, there is only one God and therefore only one final destination.

The *Kabbalah*'s teachings have given structure and meaning not only to my visions and encounters with other worlds, but also to the sacred sounds I have been taught. Through my study of *Kabbalah*, I have come to understand the spiritual principles of the universe that are the basis for the power of these sounds.

The secrets of these sacred sounds have been hidden for centuries. They are buried deep within the *Kabbalah*, in such texts as the *Sefer haZohar*, the *Tikkuney haZohar*, and the *Sefer haBahir*, as well as in such mystical writings as Gikatila's *Sha'ar haNekud*, The Gate of the Vowel Points.[5] In these writings one finds intricate descriptions of the mysteries of the sounds as well as their relationship to creation and the Kabbalistic Tree of Life.

These sacred vocal sounds bypass the intellectual constructs of the mind. They have the power to transcend gender, race, ethnicity, and personal history. Because of their universal nature, they can be used by all of us to foster spiritual growth. Eventually I developed their use in the non-verbal practice of Sound Prayer and began to use the sounds in directed and purposeful ways to bring healing and spiritual awakening to those who gathered around me.

The practice of Sound Prayer is specifically dedicated to bringing our inner knowledge into consciousness in order to awaken our *neshamah*, our higher soul. Sound Prayer involves entering a meditative state by chanting specific combinations of sacred sounds. Its power to help awaken our *neshamah* derives in large part from the fact that each of the vocal sounds made during Sound Prayer has the unique vibratory resonance of one of eight different Hebrew vowels. These sounds are each mystically tied to the holy name of God, *YHVH*,[6] and together they underlie all existence.

Sound Prayer is a heart-based practice, as opposed to an intellectual one. This does not mean that it is anti-intellectual. It is simply to say that its power comes from the yearning of our hearts rather than the reasoning of our minds. This is a crucial distinction. According to mystical teaching, spiritual awakening cannot be arrived at through intellectual reasoning alone. Thus, a practice such as Sound Prayer, which directly connects us with the forces of the universe, is critical for achieving transformative spiritual growth.

For the Kabbalist, it is no accident that the letter *Bet* (ב) which is the first letter of the Hebrew Bible, and the letter *Lamed* (ל) which is the last letter of the Hebrew Bible, spell out the Hebrew word *lev* (לב) or "heart." Nor is it to be wondered at that when God asked King Solomon, considered the wisest of men, what gift he wished to receive, the King's one request was that he be given "a hearing heart."[7]

Just as the heart has dominion over the body—without its life-blood the body and mind cannot function—so too the heart has dominion over the soul. This is underscored by the fact that in the numerology of *gematria* the value of the Hebrew word for heart is thirty-two, the number of paths that, according to the *Kabbalah*, lead to the spiritual awakening of our higher soul.

My teaching now takes me all over the world. In my travels, language is never a barrier, since Sound Prayer speaks to everyone—it is the primordial language of the soul. I have taught Sound Prayers to gatherings of terminally ill men and women in Mexico, to groups of Israeli Arabs and Jews together throughout the Holy Land, as well as spiritual seekers throughout Europe and Asia. In the United States, my work has taken me from coast to coast, and individuals from all over the world make their way to my home in upstate New York.

During all this time, my answering angel has been a constant companion, carefully leading me on a path designed to enhance my spiritual journey and deepen my wisdom through study, meditation, the correct use of ritual, and Sound Prayer. At every step, the *Kabbalah* has been a source of incomparable guidance and King Solomon's love poem has yielded up innumerable treasures. I have finally come to understand that his "Song of Songs" about the search for the love of the beautiful Shulamite is an allegory about the *Shekhinah*, the

Divine indwelling female aspect of God, and how She reveals Herself to men and women in the world.

It is a reminder that the search for the Beloved, the tender longing of the seeker, and the beauty and elusiveness of the sought are one and the same. It is the wisdom of our essential oneness. It is a wisdom that I forever hold dear to my heart, and that I am privileged to share.

2

The Curtain of Souls

BEFORE BIRTH, EACH OF us is like a thread in a divine tapestry, a "curtain of souls." The thread of our existence is interwoven with the threads of the All. Descending from the One, we are born into separation and duality. This descent and separation is a painful tearing of the fabric of our existence.

Before our soul descends into the world, we know everything there is to know; we know all the worlds, our reason for being, our destiny, and our connection to All That Is. Then, at birth, an angel touches our lips and this knowledge and our intimate connection to the Creator is forgotten. Compelled by our need for survival, we are drawn inexorably into the stream of life, focusing all our energy on obtaining nourishment, maintaining our physical safety, and mastering our earthly environment.

The angel who touches our lips and causes us to forget does not completely erase our memory. Faint awareness remains of what we once knew. Living with this subtle awareness submerged within, we sense that something important has been lost.

At the same time, there is often an unreality about this sense of loss. What could be missing? How could we begin to look for it? It is like the buried fortunes in fairy tales. The treasure has been buried so long that talk of its existence seems unbelievable. Nonetheless, despite attempts to ignore or dismiss it, memory lingers of our soul's original state of oneness. Hidden but active, this memory exerts a powerful influence. All have felt its pull at one time or another.

To reclaim the treasure of our higher soul's forgotten knowledge, and to heal our original wound of separation, we must embark upon a hero's quest to find this concealed and heavily guarded jewel. The journey beckons us, through many twists and turns, across moats filled with dark creatures and burning fires, to travel beyond the twin dragons of our ego's fear and delusion.

In most cases, this journey begins only after we have gone through the process of developing a separate sense of self, learning how to protect ourselves, physically and emotionally, from others and the world around us. Once this "growing up" takes place, our spiritual journey commences in earnest as each of us is drawn to make our way back, step-by-step, to a state of oneness and connection. In this process of awakening our higher soul, everything that has happened to us in the past and all that will happen to us in the future plays a role.

The rewards of our pilgrimage back to wholeness include the gift of uncovering our soul's unique individual purpose here on earth. It is one of the central teachings of *Kabbalah* that everything in creation has a reason for existing and each human being has a unique purpose on earth. Even if it is not apparent to us, each of us plays an essential role in the structure of the world. This is one reason why we must always have a profound reverence for all human life.

For most of us, unaware of our reason for being, life often seems empty and without meaning. Some question why they exist at all. Finding the answer to the question "Why am I here?" is one of the greatest rewards of spiritual growth.

Many, unfortunately, will succeed in forestalling their spiritual growth, with sad consequences. A stunting of spiritual development exacts a heavy price in physical illness and mental suffering. Regardless of our state of spiritual understanding, however, we are always married to the consciousness of the universe. Not metaphorically, but in a real way, we are interwoven with and inseparable from the Eternal.

The evolution of our spiritual consciousness is a continuous process of development, taking many lifetimes. We are born again and again in order to reach the full expression of our soul's unique purpose. This should not be confused with becoming a perfect being. As

humans, living in the world of duality, perfection is neither possible nor expected.

In each life, our spiritual journey does not start from
scratch, since we have our soul's lessons from countless
lives lived before. We begin life in relationship to our
past lives, with debts to pay, and rewards to reap. In
addition, the consequences of our past lives influence us
to act and react in certain ways, while at the same time
we are continuously creating new consequences from
our actions during this life. In this way, nothing that we
do, no matter how small, is without consequence.

Regardless of how ordinary our everyday reality
may seem, each of us is on this sacred journey across
our many lives. Unaware of this truth, most of us mistake the surface of our life for the essence of what it is
to be human, but underneath, the real story unfolds—
the yearning pulse of our higher soul quietly and per-
sistently beats.

In the spiritual journey across our many lives, the
destination and the Source are the same. Once we per-
ceive our oneness with God, we understand that the
Source points to the destination, and the destination
leads to the Source. This is one of the many meanings
of the teaching that "The end is embedded in the beginning and the beginning in the end, like a flame in a
burning coal."[1]

Journeying back to the One, our life is our lesson
plan. It is designed to give us the opportunity to address
unresolved issues from past incarnations, as well as to

fulfill commandments we have failed to honor. But nothing is predetermined. We are co-creators of our lives with God; as we exercise our free will, every one of our thoughts, deeds, and prayers shape our path.

Understanding that life's challenges are actually meant to be opportunities for spiritual growth, we respond to them differently. Instead of feeling angry or victimized, we are able to ask: "What is this difficult person or challenging circumstance meant to teach me?" This does not mean, however, that every person or situation we encounter is necessarily for our good. Pure evil exists in the world and serves no purpose other than its own. When we encounter it, we must forcefully seek to overcome it.

The *Kabbalah* has much to say about the existence of evil. One of the most intriguing teachings comes from the great Kabbalist, Isaac Luria, known as the Lion or *Ari*. Expanding on earlier doctrine, Luria taught that the existence of evil is an inevitable result of the creation of the world itself. Lurianic *Kabbalah* teaches that before creation, existence and God were one and the same. Nothing, including space or time, existed except the limitless being of God. This pre-creation state is, of course, impossible for the human intellect to grasp. This is because the concepts of space and time are necessary for us to conceive of anything having existence at all, including God.

This inability of our mind, however, is no fatal defect for the Kabbalist, since it is central to mystical thinking that we can only begin to apprehend certain aspects of God and creation during deep states of meditation and elevated consciousness. It is only during such states that our minds are released from the confines of ordinary logic and the limiting concepts of space and time.

Luria's mystical teaching goes on to speak of the first act of creation as God withdrawing or "contracting into Himself" in order to allow there to be a place for the world to come into being—rather like God making room for creation itself. This act of God, called *tzimtzum*, resulted in the existence of what we call space. Luria goes on to say that since this was space where God was absent, having withdrawn Himself in order for it to be, it was space that could not possibly have the quality of perfection.

This state of imperfection eventually led to *shevirah* or a "shattering of the vessels" meant to contain the light of God's subsequent creative emanations. The actual teaching is marvelously complex, but in simple terms, the image is one of God pouring His light into containers not strong enough to hold His creative force. In this cataclysm, the shards of the broken vessels gave substance to dark forces of evil which are known as *kelipot*. The *kelipot* are like "husks" or "shells" imprisoning a certain amount of the Divine light. Thus, the world was "broken" from its beginning and *Tikkun Olam*, or the repair of the world, consists of each of us working to release the trapped sparks of Divine light from their imprisonment. This is one of the most important responsibilities of every human being and is directly connected to the awakening of our higher soul.

Kabbalists speak of the soul as being comprised of five intimately connected parts, like the links on a chain: *nefesh*, the animal soul, *ruaḥ*, the spirit, *neshamah*, the higher soul, *ḥayah*, the soul's essence, and *yeḥidah*, oneness (see figure 2:1). In order to understand the relationship between these five aspects of our soul, it is helpful to imagine God as a glassblower and the soul as breath.

Think of *yeḥidah*, oneness, as existing even before the thought of making the glass. It is the force willing the glassblower's breath to arise. *Ḥayah*, the soul's essence, can be likened to the glassblower's inhalation, a focused gathering from the vast sea of oneness; it is the in-breath held before blowing. *Neshamah*, the higher soul, is akin to exhalation, the animating force of creation as it leaves the glassblower's lips. *Ruaḥ*, the spirit, is the movement of the breath as it descends through the glassblower's tube to shape the object. And finally, *nefesh*, the animal soul, is likened to the breath as it comes to rest in the created object.

The five parts of our soul are of the same essence, yet manifest differently. They exist in a kind of hierarchy, with each part aware of those below it but only intermittently aware of those above it.

The two parts of the soul that occupy the top of the hierarchy are *ḥayah*, the living essence, "the soul of the soul," which resides in the eyes, and *yeḥidah*, "one-

The Five Aspects of the Soul

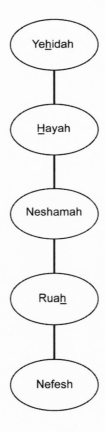

Figure 2:1

ness," which resides with God. Both exist beyond duality, outside the realm of time. Perceived by those with
elevated consciousness in lightning flashes of awareness, these parts of our soul are not influenced by
worldly events and cannot be affected by our efforts.
Nonetheless, they are part of our being and can have a
profound effect by enlightening our body once we have
reached a certain stage of spiritual development.

In contrast, every human being is born with a fully
awake and engaged *nefesh* or animal soul. Existing at
the bottom of the hierarchy, this part of us is highly
intelligent, emotional and resourceful. The main goals
of our animal soul are survival in the physical sense,
and taking care of our wants and bodily desires. To our
animal soul, everything is food, to be consumed, digest-
ed, enjoyed, hoarded, and fought over.

The animal soul lives in struggle and battle, some of it
with outside forces and much of it in a self-created civil
war between the various aspects of our personality and
desires. On this level of our being, we are constantly on
the alert, continually caught between seeking pleasure
and fleeing pain. We think only of our power and pow-
erlessness relative to the physical world around us.

Living on the level of our animal soul, our perception of ourselves rests with the external roles we perform and how successfully we perform them. We identify completely with our day to day accomplishments
and failures. We rejoice in our preferences and opinions, our loves and our hatreds, and think of our world-

ly achievements as defining who we are. The result is that for years we can fail to notice that our material successes do not provide a sense of abiding completeness and in fact often feed its opposite, an underlying loneliness and despair.

For many, this is essentially the sum total of what is, in fact, a very limited existence. This is not to say that such a life is simple or uninteresting. On the contrary, it can be complex, colorful, and quite absorbing. It is, however, in an ultimate sense, empty, unrewarding and permeated by fear of loss.

Each one of us, living only on the level of our animal soul, experiences this emptiness and longs for something more. However, at this early stage in our soul's journey we are literally trapped animals. Our longing for completion simply drives our animal soul to search ever more desperately for fulfillment in the only places it knows—in the external world of things like careers, friends, lovers, spouses, physically fit bodies, ever increasing numbers of material possessions, and ever more pleasurable physical experiences.

As long as we live our life only on the level of our animal soul, stalking the perimeter, ever on guard, the possibilities inherent in our *neshamah*, our higher soul, will elude us. This includes all perception and experience of the upper worlds. Our activities are therefore little more than simply moving around the furniture in our cage. What is called for, instead, is to open the cage door and to walk free.

This freedom begins with our yearning for something more. Perhaps we are worn down by sorrow and the cycle of longing and loss. We may have a brush with death, become bored with our toys, or find that our worldly successes suddenly lack meaning. Perhaps a vision takes hold, or we may find a teacher or a teacher may find us.

Whatever the reason, driven by the whispering of our higher soul, our yearning causes us to begin to search in earnest for what we have forgotten.

This yearning produces a stirring in that part of our soul known as *ruah*, spirit or breath. Unlike the animal soul, which is bound to the body, our spirit is capable of detaching from the physical self to search the heavens. It is this part of us that loosens from our physical body when we sleep, and flies to God in order to be secretly instructed by the angels. As it is written, "In a dream, in a night vision, as sleep falls, revelation comes to the ears of man."[2] When our animal soul is at rest, the spiritual education of the body and the mind can often take place more easily than when we are fully awake. As we develop spiritually, these lessons during sleep occur with greater frequency, and we become increasingly aware of them. This is not to say that every dream is of a divine nature. There are many personal, emotional and physical elements within most dreams, and much nonsense as well. But from time to time we are aware of a different quality to our dream, and the message, warning, or teaching it contains resonates deeply.

Sometimes during sleep we may even glimpse the future, since significant events in this world are played out beforehand in the upper worlds. Thus it is said that, "nothing happens in the world but what is made known in advance either by means of a dream or by means of a proclamation. . . . Before any event comes to pass in the world, it is announced in heaven whence it is broadcast into the world."[3] This accounts for various instances of human precognition and foreknowledge. At the same time, even after an event is proclaimed, we have the power to influence it, to soften judgement through repentance, to avert difficulties through attention, or to hasten a good result through our actions and prayers.

An increase in the stirring of our *ruah*, or spirit, is a sign that we are beginning to elevate our being. Many times we can actually feel it leading us forward. Gradually, with the help of a teacher, either human or angelic, we can come to understand that our misconceptions and false attachments bring most of our sorrow and suffering. We are like those who cannot see the distant mountain because their hands are in front of their eyes. The majestic mountain is always there; we need only move our small hands away from our eyes, and pay close attention to the call of our higher soul.

Our higher soul, or *neshamah*, is the aspect of our being directly touched by God. It cannot be humiliated, or debased, or commit an evil act, and it is that part of us that allows us to persevere during times of great trial. It is a part of us that already knows everything we need to know about our personal destiny on earth, our own unique and individual reason for being, and our connection to All That Is.

The *Torah*, or Hebrew Bible, specifically points to the existence of this higher soul in the sentence: "The Lord God *formed* the man of dust from the ground."[4] Ordinarily, the word "formed" in such a sentence would be written in the Hebrew as יצר having only one letter *Yud* (י). But in every *Torah* scroll, the word "formed" in this verse is written as וייצר with two Hebrew letters *Yud* (יי). This is the only occurrence of this unusual spelling of the word "formed" in the entire *Torah*. It is significant because in Hebrew the letter *Yud* is the abbreviation for the holy name of God. The additional *Yud* in this sentence about man's formation emphasizes the point that while humans and animals share a common physical origination and a common animal soul, only humans are given an additional *neshamah* or higher soul by God.

Our higher soul operates at an entirely different level of consciousness than any other aspect of our being, since its connection to God is direct and immediate. It has a wholly different relationship to the world and functions within an entirely different set of laws. It is through the awakening of our higher soul that we open the gates to abiding joy, freedom from fear, and fulfillment of our essential nature.

Sometimes we can sense our higher soul calling out

to us. In these moments, when we listen very carefully, it is as if God is whispering in our ear. For the most part, however, we are unaware of this hidden treasure within. It is a treasure that lies quiet and dormant, until we are guided through study, intention, yearning, and prayer to awaken it.

When we fully awaken our higher soul we live in a place of surrender, embraced by God; we neither cling to the past nor wait upon the future, since our higher soul resides in a timeless world. In this awakening, concepts and ideas about how things should be fall away. Our higher soul understands that what belongs to us comes to us, and therefore it feels neither pride nor resentment. It simply recognizes our individual place in the nature of things.

Unlike the animal soul that fears for itself and its future, constantly alert to the world's countless dangers, the *neshamah*, the higher soul, fears nothing. Its connection with the body and the ego is of an entirely different order since it carries with it the knowledge that physical death is not the end.

At the level of our higher soul, feelings exist deep within the moment, to be experienced in the now; we laugh with complete abandon and weep profoundly. The rewards of living at the level of our higher soul are the rewards of a life fully lived. We no longer turn to others with the expectation that they will repay us with things such as love, appreciation, or money. We thereby allow others to be genuinely free. Sensing that there is no price tag attached to our friendship, people gather around us for the sweetness of our energy, to bathe in the radiance that surrounds and imbues us.

As our higher soul awakens, the constructs of our personality invariably begin to loosen. In many cases, the awakening is experienced much like an earthquake. As the old ground beneath us falls away, our relationships alter as we stop participating in the old ways, for they cannot bear the scrutiny of our new awareness.

While it may appear to us that in this awakening we are becoming something different, we are actually becoming more ourselves, as our animal soul assumes its proper place. Each and every thing we lose is replaced by something much stronger and much greater, and we come to understand the words of scripture: "Those who cling to the Lord God, have eternal life in the present."[5]

As we progress on this spiritual path, it is important to keep in mind that we are given human form for a reason. It is in our physical body, with all its pleasures and pains, that we are led to the awakening of our higher soul. Our physical being must participate fully in our spiritual life, since the spiritual encompasses not only the subtle nature of our soul, but the physical and material nature of our body as well.

When our higher soul awakens, we still exist on an earthly plane and share in the pleasures and sorrows of the physical, even as we dwell with the angels and partake of the higher worlds. We continue to have the same physical obligations and the same need to tend to the body. We still have to eat, sleep, and breathe. What is different is the level of our consciousness, and hence we have an entirely different relationship to these needs. In this transformation, everything is the same, yet everything changes. As the Buddhists say: "Before enlightenment, chop the wood, carry the water; after enlightenment chop the wood, carry the water."

While we often speak of spiritual accomplishment as ascension, and the journey as a climb, we must remember that this is only a manner of speaking; it is a convenience to make the description more accessible to our mind. The spiritual and the material are both composed of divine essence; they are on a continuum, one subtle, one coarse. Both our body and our soul are creations of the Holy One, and we should never ignore, or hold in contempt, any aspect of creation. When the body is perceived as an enemy of the spiritual, we distance ourselves from God.

While the body's appetites may at times confuse us, and its demands may seem to interfere with our spiritual yearnings, it is nonetheless a great teacher with an intelligence all its own—a crucial collaborator in our spiritual journey and our higher soul's awakening.

In addition to its effect on our person, there is another aspect to the awakening of our higher soul that brings its own reward as well as responsibility. The *Kabbalah* teaches that the universe is like a giant tree with its roots in heaven and its branches here on earth.

This signifies our world is sustained by nourishment from the upper worlds. But the Tree can also be described as having its roots among us, with its branches in heaven. This illustrates that each of us affects the upper worlds by constantly feeding the branches of the Tree, for better or worse. In turn, the branches of the upper worlds rain more or less good and evil upon our own.

While the image of a tree connecting all the worlds is metaphorical, the truth behind it is not. The upper worlds are entwined with our own world, just as our spiritual aspirations are entwined with our physical bodies. The macrocosm is repeated in the microcosm. The upper worlds are as real as this one, and through the awakening of our higher soul we each have the potential to make an enormous impact on how these upper worlds affect life on earth.

As the eighteenth century Kabbalist Moses Luzzatto taught, the higher soul "ties man to the highest roots. . . ."[6] Thus, the awakening of each higher soul results in an increase in the amount of nourishment the branches of the upper worlds receive, thereby effecting the outcome of events here on earth in a more positive way. Thus, each one of us can have great influence and none are powerless.

However, like infants who cannot penetrate the mysteries of the adult world, despite the fact that these mysteries are lived out in front of it, the reality of the upper worlds will remain invisible to us until our spiritual path opens up to the higher reality.

This higher reality is multidimensional in nature, standing in sharp contrast to the narrowness of everyday life. Once awakened, the human experience becomes vast and boundless, as the awakened individual participates in a universal consciousness as broad, deep, and wide as the universe itself.

The awakening of our higher soul involves every aspect of our being. It is a deliberate and methodical process of integration, bringing the intellectual, emotional, and physical into alignment, all working in concert toward the same goal.

This growth of consciousness is often experienced as chaotic, but it is actually an orderly progression. The laws of spiritual life are the same as ordinary life. In the same way that a child cannot run before it can walk, the ladder of spiritual ascension towards the awakening of our higher soul must be climbed step-by-step; no rung can be skipped. We cannot ascend until we have integrated the lessons and meanings of each prior stage of our development. If we proceed too quickly, we run the risk of self-deception and whatever growth we achieve will be shallow and difficult to sustain. If we proceed too slowly, we suffer unduly and miss many opportunities to heal ourselves and the world.

The spiritual path can be arduous. With each step there is internal conflict and in the beginning the expanded view of reality that accompanies the soul's awakening is hard to sustain. In this challenging journey, Sound Prayer is of critical help. Because it gives voice to the language of the soul and is unencumbered by the limitations of ordinary speech, the act of Sound Prayer reminds us of what we already know. It reassures us, giving us the strength to continue on our path and the wisdom to follow the right course.

3

Cultivating the Garden

THE GARDEN OF EDEN IS a spiritual destination. It is a place within each of us, where every created being is secure, with no separation from the Divine. Male and female, heaven and earth reside there in harmony. During the course of ordinary existence we may occasionally walk in this garden in brief moments of peace, integration, and ease. But to call this place our home we must first sweep clean the streets of our nature in order to allow the subtle gifts of the upper worlds to shower down on us.

On our journey of spiritual development toward the awakening of the higher soul, one of the most important tasks is to return our ego to its rightful place as guardian rather than guard. In order to access higher realms of consciousness, it is essential that the ego take its proper place as servant, not master.

The ego is a fundamental part of the *nefesh* or animal soul. It is concerned with survival, physical pleasures, worldly success, and position in society.

Development of the ego parallels our struggle with the world during childhood. Because its emergence is rooted in our sense of being separate and apart from the rest of the world, its essential nature is one of opposition and duality. It is the part of us that constantly battles to sustain the delusion that we are self-contained beings, separate from each other and God.

Beginning as a protector in our early search to find pleasure and avoid pain, it invariably becomes a despotic guard, "protecting" us from inner wisdom, casting a long shadow and hiding our true nature.

Once its kingdom is established, the ego retains a tremendous hold on us throughout our adult life, resisting all incursions against its sovereignty. Constantly on guard, it lashes out whenever its view of reality is challenged. This is especially true if the challenge comes as a result of our spiritual development, for our ego understands that every step on the path toward the awakening of our higher soul and reunion with the Holy One will mean a reduction of its power. When we resist our higher soul's call, our ego is most frequently the cause.

The ego loves accolades, fears criticism, revels in pride of ownership, and is attached to worldly possessions. Eventually, its web of delusions can become so tightly woven that almost no light can shine through. It needs little encouragement to become an inner terrorist, constantly sabotaging the soul's efforts at liberation and setting up innumerable obstacles to block spiritual development. These include deep-seated feelings of guilt and unworthiness, a false worldview, and anxiety that spiritual growth will mean a loss of worldly pleasures.

The ego's defense system is designed to convince us that any deviation from the ordinary and accepted puts us in serious jeopardy. Invariably, it grows heady with its might and begins to lord it over us like a petty dictator, prodigiously defending the status quo. Since growth and evolution are the natural order of life, our ego can bring us great suffering by refusing change and trying to hold on to things just as they are.

All the while, as it seeks to maintain control, our ego is aware that at any moment every one of its cherished worldly achievements and possessions can be taken away—by acts of nature, by our own mistakes, by those who are stronger, smarter or more cunning, or ultimately by God. Fundamentally, it exists in a state of terror, accounting for much of our emotional struggle and pain.

Above all else, the ego fears annihilation. While the annihilation of the ego is much sought after in a number of spiritual traditions, it is not a positive spiritual goal. It is a violent act that causes the instincts and emotions of our animal soul to actually increase in intensity. This, more often than not, results in behavior that is the very opposite of that for which we are striving. Attempting to destroy the ego and completely deny the needs of our animal soul is counterproductive. Such an attempt invariably causes our ego to lash out like a caged beast, resulting in our acting in ways harmful to ourselves and others.

Our ego must be transformed, not destroyed, and this process must be conducted with great care. We must give our animal nature comfort and proceed slowly. Moving too quickly produces ungrounded spiritual advances, built on shallow foundations likely to collapse.

The most appropriate place to begin this process is with an objective examination of our thoughts, speech and actions; for it is through ethical behavior and right thinking that we can best lay the foundation from which to gradually chip away at the ego structures working to keep our *neshamah*, our higher soul, from awakening. This is what is meant when it is said that the *neshamah* is clothed by the *nefesh*, our animal soul, and that the *nefesh* in turn is clothed by thought, speech, and action.[1]

In order to assist the process of the ego's transformation, it is important to understand the ways in which our ego seeks to maintain control. Guilt is one of the ego's most insidious tools in its battle against our attempts to elevate ourselves and awaken our higher soul. It is an emotion that easily exists alongside the very behavior that causes it. Feelings of guilt actually give us permission not to change, just so long as we suffer enough emotionally. Feeling guilty while continuing to think, speak, and act badly is an all too familiar pattern.

On the other hand, if we do change our behavior out of guilt, we do so grudgingly and our relationship to the old way of being is never really severed. For this reason, guilt is a selfish emotion; it has mainly to do with how we feel about ourselves, with little to do about how our behavior affects others. Unchecked, it can easily turn into morbidity and self-loathing—poisoning our life, and the lives of those around us.

In overcoming feelings of guilt, it is important to understand that we sin only out of ignorance, when we are seized by "the spirit of folly,"[2] and that "no earthly being is so righteous as to always do good, and never sin."[3] This is why guilt, and the self-hatred that often accompanies it, serves no purpose.

Maintaining a cycle of guilt and self-recrimination, the ego forestalls our spiritual growth by making us feel unworthy to attain it. Sound Prayer closes the door on guilt and opens the door for repentance as it reminds us of our intrinsic self-worth as part of creation.

Repentance is a state of mind entirely different from guilt. Repentance is not about blame or self-flagellation. Instead, it is an openhearted recognition of the effects of our negative thoughts, speech, and actions. It involves recognizing the true nature of our failings, taking responsibility for them, sincerely attempting not to repeat them, and making amends where possible. In this way, we detach from the past and begin to heal in the present. Real forgiveness of the self and of others becomes possible, releasing energy for life and growth.

This type of forgiveness can only result from compassion for the human condition, compassion for our own emotional neediness and confusion, and compassion for our own rash and blind actions committed out of ignorance. It is a compassion that arises from realizing the impossibility of always behaving correctly and of always knowing the right thing to do. It is a compassion that arises when we accept the difficulty of reconciling the physical, emotional, intellectual, and spiritual aspects of our being. Through such compassion, we invariably come to humility and forgiveness of self. It is only through self-forgiveness, and full acceptance of our human failings, that we are able to have genuine compassion for others.

In the course of a fully lived life, every human being will do things that are wrong and that harm themselves and others. Some of the harm will be irreparable, impossible to undo in one lifetime. The capacity for repentance and forgiveness is what allows us to continue our spiritual development despite our imperfections. It is God's great gift of redemption.

The ego is also a master of deceit. It continually attempts to cultivate a false worldview focused on the centrality of the individual and the belief that material possessions and worldly success define who we are. At the height of its control, it constantly violates the commandment "Thou shall have no other gods before me,"⁴ as it elevates the false gods of status, position, and power to a place of worship.

Awakening our higher soul requires a willingness to abandon false gods and to discard the idea that we are the titles we hold, the status we have, or the income we receive. These attachments play a large role in keeping us spiritually asleep. While power, position, and wealth may win for us temporary admiration and acceptance in the eyes of others, if they are all we have we will invariably come to the sobering realization that we have little of lasting value.

The ego is also responsible for the false view that the nature of spiritual life is one of asceticism and self-denial. In fact, the nature of the spiritual has nothing to do with these, for our bodies and our pleasures are God-given, and He loves our laughter and our songs.

In addition, the ego is an expert at manipulation, and fear is one of its most effective tools. When the tentacles of fear attach themselves, they are extremely difficult to detach. Even when, through great effort, we remove them from our mind, they often come to rest in the body, causing pain and illness. For this reason, overcoming deep-seated fear is something we must do carefully.

Fear does have a role in our lives, warning us of impending physical danger. Its essential nature, however, is one of contraction of both the physical and spiritual bodies. Fear manifests as conformity, forced behavior, and the avoidance of responsibility. It produces suffering similar to taking a growing organism and putting it into a too-small box.

It is also responsible for much of the emotional constriction of our heart, inoculating us against feelings of caring and hence a full experience of life. Fear is also often the cause of hatred and irrational anger, both of which lie at the root of much violence, often directed against imagined dangers. Whenever we experience fear, we owe it to ourselves to look deep inside our soul to determine its true source.

The ego's desire to be in complete control, and its belief that we alone determine our fate, is another roadblock to spiritual development. It is important to understand that no matter what efforts we make, or what path we follow, our progress is determined by our relationship to our Creator as well as our interactions with the world of the angels. This is a realization with far-reaching consequences.

The understanding that we are eternally connected to God, that we are not alone in our struggles, and that the fabric of our existence is intertwined with the beings of the angelic world, literally opens up entire new realms. It is an understanding that transforms our path from a simple struggle for emotional and physical security into one that is truly meaningful and ennobling.

Sound Prayer can be instrumental in helping us arrive at this understanding. It affords us an opportunity to experience the *Shekhinah*, God's indwelling female Presence on earth. While our experience of the

Shekhinah during Sound Prayer is usually momentary, its effect is deeply reassuring, freeing us from impatience and pretense. The sweetness of the *Shekhinah*'s Presence resonates within our being, causing us to yearn for Her continual embrace. Over time, the experience brings a sense of something completely new attempting to emerge—it is the Divine Presence that dwells within slowly revealing itself.

The commitment to cleave to God, combined with the practice of Sound Prayer, coupled with the right attitude towards our thought, speech, and action, can completely transform our ego and dissolve its tyranny. This transformative process may be experienced at first as a kind of loss, with attendant mourning. But if we proceed carefully, as aspects of our ego transform, we find a fresh source of energy and a freer, more expanded sense of self. Negative attachments, problems, and delusions of our prior state of consciousness fall away. The experience becomes not one of annihilation, but of revelation.

The result is that guilt disappears, false opinions reduce their hold on us, fear begins to evaporate, and gentleness prevails. We come to understand that suffering is largely self-inflicted, resulting from wanting what we cannot have, trying to possess what does not belong to us, and believing that we can be deeply satisfied by what cannot satisfy.

4

Angels

KABBALISTS REFER TO THE world of the angels as *Olam haYetzirah* or the World of Formation. Angels, called *malakhim* in Hebrew, are inextricably entwined with our daily lives and play an essential role in spiritual development. Every human being experiences them in one form or another—they are real and present beings, far from imaginary.

Angels are created either by God, as His agents and messengers, or by each of us as a result of our deeds. Some exist for a brief moment, others are allowed by God to exist for long periods. In all cases each angel serves only a single purpose at a time during its existence.

Many of the angels who serve as God's agents are sent to us in response to our prayers and our spiritual yearning. In this way, angels are a bridge between earthly existence and God. To emphasize this aspect of the angelic world, the *Tikkuney haZohar* points out that *gematria* ascribes the number ninety-one to the Hebrew word for "angel."[1] The significance of this is that ninety-one is also the number arrived at by adding together twenty-six, the number given to *YHVH*, the transcendental and holiest name of God, and sixty-five, which is the number given by *gematria* to *Adonai*, God's earthly name used in prayer.

Unlike God's angelic messengers, the angels we ourselves create come directly from our deeds, good and bad. Surrounding us, they draw good or bad fortune to us until their measure is exhausted. Thus, each of our actions has implications for us beyond their impact on others. As the *Zohar* tells us, no act is without consequence and "In truth, a man by his actions is always drawing to himself some emissary of the other world, good or evil, according to the path he treads."[2] This phenomenon is somewhat akin to the concept of karma.

The angels we create ourselves do not manifest in physical form. Their essential nature is experienced as an urge, impulse, or inclination. Interaction with these angels is very much like an ongoing inner dialogue. Having come into existence as a result of our thoughts and actions, they in turn influence our subsequent thoughts and actions for good or evil. As we grow older, it is increasingly difficult to ignore the angels we create, since our thoughts and behaviors have created them in ever-greater numbers.

In addition to the angels we create, it is said in the

Zohar that two angels accompany each of us throughout our life, whispering into our ears.[3] One, an agent of
Yetzer haTov, the force of good, prompts us in the right
direction but stands aside when we choose to cooperate
with the forces of darkness. The other angel, an agent
of *Yetzer haRah*, the force of evil, prompts us toward
wickedness. Using ego and pride as its instrument, and
satisfaction of the senses as bait, it encourages us in our
decisions to obey the beckoning voice of evil inclination. In the end, however, the choice is always ours.
Angels help to determine our fate, but in this we are not
passive. They are guides but never masters.

Sound Prayer, through the stirring of our higher soul,
reduces our inclination toward evil and creates a longing for peace, love, and fulfillment through union with
the Creator. This longing to attune and harmonize with
the One is received by the Creator as an offering from
our heart. The beings of the world of angelic messengers ready themselves to receive and transmit this offering. In this way our vibrations are carried upward, and
then returned to us in the form of a memory of our
inseparability from God.

At the same time, it is important to understand that
angels serve only as God's agents and do not have a will
of their own. As messengers of the Holy One and servants of a higher purpose, they can do nothing unless
God first decrees it. This is why, while we can seek
God's protection in the form of an angelic presence, we
should never address our prayers to angels themselves.

In Hebrew Holy Scripture, angels are often described as having human form, appearing many times to impart lessons, render guidance, or bring retribution. Such beings have a deep hold on the human psyche. The stories that portray human-like angels interacting with biblical characters are often meant to describe the actual role of the angelic world in our everyday lives. The biblical story of Jacob and his battle with an angel is a case in point.

In his youth, Jacob deceived his father Isaac, stealing the blessing that belonged to Esau his brother and firstborn son. Years later, the stage is set for a violent confrontation between the two men. In the lead up to this battle, Esau is accompanied by a force of 400 men, while Jacob is traveling in the company of mostly women and children.

The night before the conflict between the brothers, an angel accosts Jacob and the two of them wrestle until morning. At daybreak the angel withdraws, leaving Jacob exhausted but undefeated. This contest between Jacob and the angel ends up taking the place of the physical battle between Jacob and his brother; a battle that surely would have resulted in Jacob's death. Instead, the next morning Esau extends his hand to Jacob in peace.

This story reveals that, sometimes, difficult experiences are sent by God to serve as a substitute for much harsher or more dangerous experiences. As we awaken our higher soul, we are increasingly able to identify these angelic interventions in our lives. As a result, we become increasingly motivated to alter our behavior in order to merit them.

The biblical story of Jacob's battle with the angel teaches another spiritual lesson. Before withdrawing, the angel wounds Jacob on the thigh. After Jacob is wounded, the angel gives him the new name of *Israel*. In Hebrew, this means both "princely" and "struggle with God" and for Jacob, it signifies the next stage in his spiritual development. The wound to Jacob's thigh makes Jacob "walk" a different path, and his life is rededicated to God.

The lesson here is that spiritual transformation is often accompanied by a physical transformation brought about by the forces of the angelic world. Importantly, sometimes this physical change is very much like a wound, and the awakening that accompanies it may not be immediately apparent to us. Indeed, sometimes the wound is a sign that the awakening itself portends additional struggle, as in the case of the newly named *Israel* and his descendants.

Another Biblical example of the connection between a physical wound and spiritual growth is the story of Isaiah and his experience of God seated upon a throne in all His glory. Isaiah immediately perceives himself to be in grave danger, thinking himself unworthy to be in God's presence. He cries out to God in fear: "I am a man of unclean lips, and I live in the midst of a people of unclean lips."[4]

Upon uttering these words, an angel flies to Isaiah's side with a burning coal and touches it to his lips, saying, "This has touched your lips; and your sins are cast out."[5] Once again, a wound serves as a sign of spiritual ascension, as well as purification and absolution. In addition, it marks the beginning of Isaiah's long struggle to fulfill his God-appointed task of bringing the people of Israel back to righteousness.

Understanding the role of angels in shaping our destiny is an important part of spiritual growth. We cannot see the world of the angels with normal vision, nor can we apprehend angels with minds that are overly preoccupied with worldly concerns. However, through the gift of Sound Prayer, we are given the opportunity to experience their presence directly, disclosing what cannot be seen otherwise. This "seeing" reminds us that we are not alone in our struggles, and that we are all accompanied by God's servants on our journey of awakening.

At the same time, it is imperative to understand that the more we awaken our higher soul, the more we attract beings from the entire spiritual realm. For in addition to angels, there exist innumerable other spiritual entities, many of whom can have a negative influence on the human mind. As the great Kabbalist Joseph Gikatila wrote, the universe is "filled with battalions and multitudes. Some are pure and merciful and some are impure and harming. All are standing and flying in the air; there is no free space between heaven and earth."[6]

Spirits of chaos are always waiting for an opportunity to throw dust into our eyes and confuse us with false arguments. This is why our spiritual development must proceed carefully with no rung on the ladder of the Tree of Life skipped; all the lessons of each rung must be completely integrated before proceeding to the next. Only the path of compassion, humility, decency, and spiritual caution can protect us from evil. Therefore, we must prepare ourselves fully—physically, emotionally, and mentally—before taking the next step on the ladder and opening additional doors to the worlds above.

5

The Names of God

OUR EXILE FROM THE paradise of the Garden of Eden means that each of us must find our individual way back into God's presence.

At the beginning of each life, we all start out with at least some experience of the Holy One, some sense of the Creator. From this beginning, as well as our early religious teachings, we derive our initial ideas, fears, and hopes about God.

As time goes on, our thoughts and emotions about God invariably change. As we grow up, some of us lose faith altogether. However, for those of us who continue to seek, there comes a gradual and purposeful awakening of our higher soul.

Along the way, each soul witnesses and experiences many different levels of God's revelation; we reach to God as God reaches to us. At any given time, however, we are only capable of perceiving His light according to our personal level of spiritual development. God appears in our lives in many different ways according to our ability to understand. This is the meaning behind God's statement to Moses in the *Torah*: "I am the Lord, and I appeared to Abraham, to Isaac, and to Jacob, by the name of *El-Shaddai*, but by my name *YHVH*, I was not made known to them."[1]

The Hebrew Holy Scripture contains many different God names. God's use of these different names is a way of showing that The Infinite One discloses Itself to us at various times through a variety of religious experiences, with each God name representing a different level of spiritual understanding and awareness. This "veiling of the Countenance"[2] reflects the fact that God is not a fixed, unchanging being in our lives; His presence is dynamic and our understanding of Him evolves over time.

El-Shaddai, the name by which God appeared to the patriarchs Abraham, Isaac, and Jacob, is related to some of our very earliest feelings about God. In Hebrew, there is a term *el shaddai*, which is written with the same letters as the God name but with different vowel points, and which means "toward my (female) breasts." This illustrates that there is an aspect to *El-Shaddai*, the God of the patriarchs, that is protective and nurturing. At the same time, there is another side to *El-Shaddai*, which is illuminated when we separate the word *Shaddai* into the Hebrew words *shad* and *dai*. The Hebrew word for demon is *shed*, which is written with the same letters as *shad*, and the Hebrew word *dai* means "enough."

Thus, *El-Shaddai* also has to do with the limits and boundaries between the natural and the supernatural. This separation was a necessity for the people of Abraham, Isaac, and Jacob's time. For these early men and women, there needed to be a clear division between themselves and the unseen worlds, between the world of the finite and the incomprehensible realm of the infinite Creator. Theirs was an abiding fear of the forces of the other worlds. It was a fear of getting too close to God, of looking upon His countenance, of being consumed by His fire.

This historical reality is recapitulated in our individual spiritual development. At certain times in our lives most of us experience God in a way similar to the ancient Hebrews. We are fearful of the unseen—of "getting too close," and of "being consumed." We seek comfort by creating barriers between the Divine and ourselves.

The God name *Elohim*, first encountered in the creation story in Genesis, is closely connected with *El-Shaddai*. *Elohim* is the God name most associated with the destruction of wars, the ravages of storms, and the curse of human suffering. *Elohim* is the God of our animal soul. He is, first and foremost, a giver of reward and punishment, an entity with whom we bargain and negotiate. *Elohim* is the harsh, punitive God who watches our every move. As it is written, "Judgement is for *Elohim*."[3]

Our relationship with *Elohim* involves the offering of trades, the use of intermediaries, and the fear of retribution. In some ways, this is God as simply a more powerful version of ourselves, a God of immanence rather than transcendence. It is possible for us to spend an entire lifetime with *Elohim* as the only God we know.

The four letter God name *Y-H-V-H* (י-ה-ו-ה), called the Tetragrammaton, is of an entirely different order. It is forbidden for any to speak this name out loud, and we have no way of knowing for certain how it was originally pronounced.[4] The prohibition against pronouncing the name *YHVH* is an acknowledgement of its profoundly sacred nature. When the God name *YHVH* occurs in a Hebrew prayer book, the name *Adonai* is spoken in its place, or one may pronounce each Hebrew letter separately as *Yud, Hay, Vav, Hay*. If one wishes to refer to it in ordinary discourse, one substitutes the word *Hashem*, which simply means "the Name."

YHVH is timeless, above and beyond nature. In Hebrew, the letters *Y-H-V-H*, rearranged, spell the word "existence." They are also letters that make up the Hebrew words for "was," "is," and "will be." Unknowable and unpronounceable, *YHVH* encompasses all aspects of the Godhead. As the great thirteenth century Kabbalist Joseph Gikatila wrote, "Know that all the Holy Names in the *Torah* are intrinsically tied to the four letter name of God, the *YHVH*. *YHVH* is the trunk of the tree that nurtures the branches which spread to every side, which are the other names of God, and each one of these branches, which is a Holy Name, bears a different fruit."[5]

The four letters making up the Tetragrammaton are extremely powerful and can be used to enter deep meditative states. Visualizing the entire name, reciting the letters individually and combining them with certain vowel sounds, one can begin to feel the mystery of its creative force. It appears and disappears, requiring ever greater concentration to keep it from receding completely. In this way, the force of the Holy One is revealed, yet not approached.

YHVH is the God of our higher soul, and through His mercy and compassion all of the other God names are completed. Since the higher soul expresses the unique purpose of each individual, its relationship to *YHVH* is one of fulfillment. *YHVH* is where we begin to find peace through the acceptance of the incomprehensible in life, the mystery and splendor of the universe. It is where our yearning for unity and transcendence is heard and received.

YHVH brings balance to a world that cannot endure on the basis of the strict judgement of *Elohim* alone. This is why when the *Torah* speaks of the completion of creation, it refers to God as "*YHVH Elohim*" in the sentence: "These are the chronicles of the heaven and the earth when they were created, on the day that the *Lord God* made earth and the heavens."[6] The joining of *YHVH* and *Elohim* together into the combined name,

"Lord God," shows us that after God finished creating the world, it contained both aspects of His being.

The God name *Ein Sof*, the "Limitless One," differs from all others in that it is a name without being a name. It is God, unknowable and unfathomable, neither masculine nor feminine. We cannot ascribe any qualities to *Ein Sof*. It is the Mystery beyond the worlds, the endless beginning, the beginningless end, and the *Ilat haIlot*, the "Cause of all Causes."

Ein Sof cannot be approached or prayed to—there exists no line of communication to *Ein Sof*. Its incomprehensible light is hidden from all; even from the most advanced. There are certain things that can never be known. Instead, we experience the judgement of *Elohim*, the protection of *El-Shaddai*, the unconditional love of *YHVH*, and, in prayerful meditation and flashes of insight, the presence of the *Shekhinah*, the indwelling female aspect of God.

The journey from *El-Shaddai* and *Elohim* to *YHVH* and *Ein Sof* is a journey from belief to faith. The difference between belief and faith is that belief can be taught, while faith must be earned. What we are taught is something handed to us, a description of the world, a "belief system." Faith, on the other hand, we carve from our own experience, from our own pain. Those who have been sorely tested either achieve a deeper faith or abandon faith altogether. In the realm of faith, what we earn through effort and what is sustained through periods of doubt is often unbreakable.

Faith is the basis of all mystical understanding. When as men and women we come into true faith, it is well grounded and deeply rooted, for we have purchased it with experience, with joy, with tragedy, and with sorrow. Most important, and above all, we have come to it freely and willingly.

When our faith is deeply rooted and built on a solid foundation, it is not annihilated by evil and suffering, nor does it quake before that which is fearsome. Instead it perceives hardship and struggle as another face of the Almighty. Faith gives us the courage to continue our spiritual journey despite cruelty and pain.

Only the most committed of souls stay the course, and only the blessed make it to the final destination. There, the angels step aside and the sword that guards the Tree of Life turns its blade to allow the passage of the righteous. This marks the journey from the simple faith of a small child to the belief of the adult, and then back again to faith.

6

The Tree of Life

THE KABBALAH TEACHES THAT God created the universe with vibrations.[1] These vibrations became the foundation of everything that is, bringing into the world different aspects of the Divine nature.

In the empty space that existed before creation, these vibrations took form as ten emanations, or *Sefirot*. Within *Kabbalah* there are many levels of explanation as to the nature of the *Sefirot*, and no single description can encompass the totality of their being.

One way to think of them is as the ten fundamental organizing principles of the world. Because each individual *Sefirah* corresponds to a different one of God's creative vibrations, each represents a different aspect of God's creative force as it cascades, in levels of concealment and revelation, toward its manifestation here on earth. Since creation is not a one-time event, but rather an ongoing process, the forces of the *Sefirot* act continuously, both within the world and within each of us. In this way, every human being is a co-creator of reality with God.

Together the *Sefirot* form the Kabbalistic Tree of Life or *Etz Haim* (see figure 6.1). This structure is more than just a convenient way to organize the various *Sefirot*. Combined with a proper understanding of the nature of the *Sefirot* and their relationship to each other, the Tree of Life becomes a roadmap, leading to an intimate connection with the Holy One.

The individual names of the ten *Sefirot* are *Keter*, *Hokhmah*, *Binah*, *Gedullah*, *Gevurah*, *Tiferet*, *Netzah*, *Hod*, *Yesod*, and *Malkhut*.

These names are derived from two verses in Holy Scripture and each name is a description of the quality of the *Sefirah* it names. The two Biblical verses are: "I have filled him with the spirit of God (*Keter*), with wisdom (*Hokhmah*), with understanding (*Binah*) . . ."[2] and "Thine, O God are the Greatness (*Gedullah*), the Strength (*Gevurah*), the Beauty (*Tiferet*) the Eternity (*Netzah*) and the Splendor (*Hod*) for All (*Yesod*) in heaven and in earth; Thine, O God is the Kingdom (*Malkhut*)."[3]

Although the *Sefirot* can be thought of as giving material shape to God's creation, they should not be thought of as in any way similar to the everyday objects that make up our world. They have no tangible physical properties in and of themselves, nor are they energy centers or objects to be worshiped.

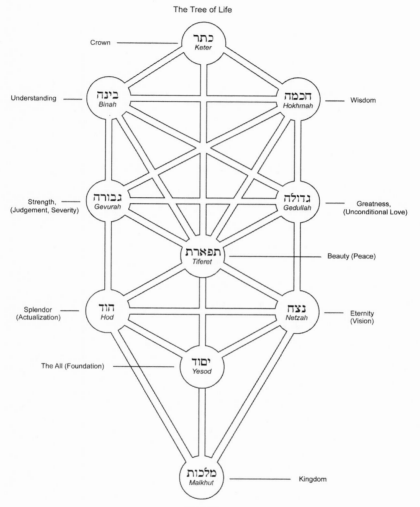

The Tree of Life

Crown — כתר / Keter

Understanding — בינה / Binah

Wisdom — חכמה / Hokhmah

Strength, (Judgement, Severity) — גבורה / Gevurah

Greatness, (Unconditional Love) — גדולה / Gedullah

תפארת / Tiferet — Beauty (Peace)

Splendor (Actualization) — הוד / Hod

נצח / Netzah — Eternity (Vision)

The All (Foundation) — יסוד / Yesod

Kingdom — מלכות / Malkhut

Figure 6:1

Instead, their combined essence can be thought of as a blueprint that reflects how the universe actually is, as opposed to the way we imagine it or would like it to be. In addition, because we are created in God's image, these ten aspects of the divine are also part of our human nature. In this way, the various aspects of the *Sefirot* reflect the intellectual, emotional, and physical basis for how we relate to ourselves, to each other, to the physical world around us, and ultimately to God.

Although they do not have the physical properties of the world that they themselves were instrumental in creating, the *Sefirot* nonetheless have real existence. Gifted mystics, in moments of great concentration, can visualize them for brief moments and the more we incorporate the vibrations of Sound Prayer into our lives, the deeper will become our comprehension of the multidimensional nature of the *Sefirot*.

Specific Sound Prayers can be used to create channels called *tzinnorot* in order to connect the various *Sefirot* to each other. The creation of these channels through Sound Prayer serves to bring balance into our lives, helping to end the constant internal struggles and civil war within us. This allows us to start hearing the still, quiet voice of our own higher wisdom as it seeks to foster the awakening of our higher soul. These channels also help in bringing about *Tikkun Olam*, or the repair of our world, by rejoining that which has been separated.

In addition to comprising the Kabbalistic Tree of Life, the ten *Sefirot* are often shown arrayed on a mystical being called *Adam Kadmon*, or Primordial Man. This formation highlights the *Sefirot*'s relationship to the human body (see figure 6.2).

The specific placement of the *Sefirot* on *Adam Kadmon* organizes them into three categories—intellectual, emotional, and physical—with the *Sefirot* from each category occupying a different segment of the body. The physical is expressed primarily from the genitals to the waist, the emotional from the waist to the throat, and the intellectual from the throat upwards.

While each *Sefirah* is separate and distinct, they are meant to function in a balanced relationship to each other. In most of us, however, the qualities of certain *Sefirot* tend to dominate, and we each tend to cultivate the traits of particular *Sefirah* at the expense of others. Spiritual development requires that we work toward the correct balance of each *Sefirah* in ourselves and in the world. This is one of the most important purposes of Sound Prayer.

Keter

The first and most exalted of the *Sefirot* is *Keter* (Crown): On *Adam Kadmon*, *Keter* is visualized just above the head. It can be thought of as the *Sefirah* through which the light of all creation continuously flows. Unapproachable, unknowable, impossible to

Adam Kadmon: Primordial Man

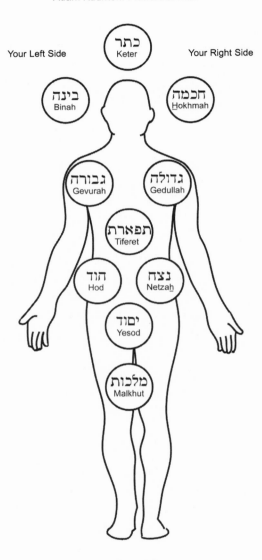

Figure 6:2

grasp, it is the emanation that enables the Tree of Life, and therefore the world, to exist.

We know *Keter* only through what it represents, which is constant creation. It relates to God's description of Himself in the Hebrew Bible as an ever-present creative force of continuous becoming, expressed in the words "I Will Be That Which I Will Be,"[4] often mistranslated from the Hebrew as "I Am That I Am."

With a simple rearrangement of the vowel points in the letters of the word *keter* we have the Hebrew word *kitur* meaning "to surround," as God's Presence surrounds everything.

Rabbi Na<u>h</u>man of Bratzlov, an eighteenth century mystic, translates *Keter* as the admonition to "be ready." *Keter* demands from each of us that we be fully alive in order to be ready to receive God's teaching with wisdom (<u>*H*</u>*okhmah*) and to act with understanding (*Binah*).

The force of *Keter* constantly presses upon us, urging us to be eternally open to the present moment and to allow the generative force of the Creator to flow unimpeded through each of the other *Sefirot* during Sound Prayer. These generative forces find their final destination in the *Sefirah Malkhut*, which represents the sum of who we are individually and collectively.

Another rearrangement of the vowels in the Hebrew letters that make up the word *keter* gives us the Hebrew word *karet*, which means "cut off." This illustrates that individuals who misuse the forces of creation for their own personal aggrandizement, or those who approach the mysteries of creation without sufficient preparation, face the prospect of being cut off or severed from their connection to God. Thus, great suffering awaits the spiritually arrogant, for there is no greater despair than being cut off from God's light and plunged into darkness.

Hokhmah

Hokhmah (Wisdom) is visualized on the right side of the head of *Adam Kadmon*. One way to think of *Hokhmah* is as an enlightened state of mind, a place of clear knowing, of knowing without knowing how you know. *Hokhmah* is pure and direct seeing, and it sits closest to the crown of *Keter*.

An individual experiencing *Hokhmah* consciousness apprehends everything in creation through immediate awareness, without the encumbrances of human needs, wants, desires, or personal opinions.

The wisdom of *Hokhmah* is non-verbal and non-conceptual. Like water, it has no form of its own and cannot be used unless contained by something other than itself. *Hokhmah*'s "container" is the *Sefirah Binah*, which serves its highest purpose by functioning in this way.

Hokhmah is the jumping off point to the other realms—the upper worlds of the palaces and of paradise, the worlds of the angels and the mysteries of creation. It is a place of pure vibration and undifferentiated sound, a place of non-dual experience from which spiritual energy, capable of curing physical suffering and illness, emerges.

It is impossible for a human being to remain in a state of *Hokhmah* consciousness for very long. Even the most spiritually advanced must gather its fruits quickly before returning to ordinary consciousness in what the *Kabbalah* refers to as the act of "running and returning."[5]

The *Sefirah Hokhmah* exists outside the realm of time, in the endless beginning, and in the infinity before the end. It has the potential to reveal what is concealed. A rearrangement of the letters of the word *Hokhmah*, results in the Hebrew words *koah mah*, translated by Kabbalists as "the power of What." This is the power and energy of everything that has the potential to come into existence, representing not just what is, but whatever will be.

During Sound Prayer, the wisdom inherent in *Hokhmah* enables us, in flashes of enlightenment, to turn away from deluded ideas about self-protection and, over time, it allows us to transform our ideas about conflict and struggle. Understood simply on the level of survival, conflict leads only to fear of the outcome. Viewed as the ground from which the essence of one's nature arises, conflict can actually reveal God's beauty, elevating our being and our lives, thereby transmuting the everyday into the sublime.

Binah

Binah (Understanding) is visualized on the left side of the head of *Adam Kadmon*. It can be thought of as the *Sefirah* of human beliefs and ideas expressed through speech and action. In its simplest form it constitutes our understanding of the "ways of the world" developed from ordinary everyday experiences. *Binah*, however, has a second and higher aspect.

In order to use the wisdom of *Hokhmah* consciousness, we must bring its clear knowing into *Binah*, thereby giving *Hokhmah*'s non-conceptual wisdom both form and expression. In this sense, *Hokhmah* may be likened to the vision of a gifted sculptor who looks at a block of marble and "sees" not the block, but rather the shape of the sculpture within it. *Binah* can then be thought of as the sculptor's ability to skillfully chip away at the extraneous matter of the block, giving the vision form, and revealing the object inside.

In this way *Binah* functions as the "container" for the wisdom of *Hokhmah*, since *Binah* is necessary for the wisdom of *Hokhmah* to have form. This is why *Hokhmah* and *Binah* are often referred to in the *Kabbalah* as father and mother.

Binah is also referred to as the place where the Throne of God is located, the place from which God expresses concern for His creation. All understanding comes from God, and it is within *Binah* that God "lowers" Himself so that He can be accessible to us.

Gedullah

As the *Bahir* teaches, *Gedullah* (Unconditional Love) is associated with the biblical patriarch Abraham. Abraham, a direct descendant of Noah, is also, through his sons Isaac and Ishmael, the father of both the Jewish and the Arab peoples. According to the prophet Mikhah, God Himself gave Abraham the attribute of kindness,[6] and the Hebrew Bible devotes several passages to his acts of generosity and thoughtfulness to strangers.[7]

The nature of *Gedullah* is to seek no explanation and to give without reason, uncritically and without questions or condition. Visualized beneath the shoulder of *Adam Kadmon* on the right side of the heart, it is related to the right arm and hand.

Gedullah is the open palm of generosity that asks nothing in return. Its energy flows directly in an endless stream from the eternal source, untouched by worldly concerns. At one with its object, it is a continuous flow of love that kindles a longing to stay forever in its embrace. It is the very opposite of the separation and loneliness that we often feel in our normal state of consciousness.

Gedullah is the pure joy of seeing beauty everywhere and in everything. As such, it is the propulsive force that enables our spiritual yearning to flow upward to the Creator. *Gedullah*, like *Hokhmah*, is a door to the infinite, for it is through love of the Creator and the creation that we gain entry to the mysteries.

The experience of *Gedullah* during Sound Prayer can cause us to literally grow faint, as the intense beauty and purity of its unconditional love overwhelms us with a sense of the ineffable.

Gevurah

Gevurah (Strength) is also called *Din*, or Judgement, and it is visualized on *Adam Kadmon* on the left side of the heart. Associated with the left arm and hand, it is the place of the warrior and the judge.

Gevurah represents stern decision and unyielding verdict rendered without feeling or emotion. It is judgement based on strict principles from which no deviation is tolerated. Accepting no excuse and offering no clemency, it allows no explanation or interpretation.

This attribute of strict judgement is a characteristic of the Divine and thus a characteristic of human nature as well. Pretending that we are not judgemental, by trying to suppress all such feelings, leads to the twin evils of untruth and hypocrisy. On the other hand, an overemphasis on the qualities of *Gevurah*, untempered by the mercy of *Gedullah*, engenders evil.

The *Kabbalah* associates the absolute and strict judgement of *Gevurah* with the biblical patriarch Isaac, who is described in the Hebrew Bible as one who feared God.[8] Commenting on the nature of fear, the *Bahir* says "It is chaos, emanating from evil which confounds,"[9] that is, to the extent that the judgement of *Gevurah* is absolute, it has the potential to create chaos.

Gevurah can be a source of harshness, chaos, and evil. Yet, in its proper relationship with the *Sefirah* of unconditional love, *Gedullah*, it becomes a place of self-restraint and discipline. At the same time, *Gevurah* is needed to constrain the unconditional love of *Gedullah*, which by itself is incapable of discriminating between good and bad, and therefore needs *Gevurah* to balance it. Thus the qualities of both *Gevurah* and *Gedullah* combined are necessary for the proper functioning of the world.

Tiferet

Tiferet (Beauty) is visualized in the middle of the body of *Adam Kadmon*, at the solar plexus. Sometimes referred to as the sun for its centrality on primordial man, it is where harmony and peace reside. Since "truth is nothing but the attribute of peace,"[10] *Tiferet* is associated with the Biblical patriarch Jacob, who was a man of peace, "a complete man,"[11] to whom God "gave truth."[12]

The location identified by *Tiferet*'s placement on *Adam Kadmon*, is the part of us from which our *ruaḥ*, or spirit, detaches while we sleep, flying to the heavens to be instructed by the angels. While most of our dreams are not touched by God in this way, from time to time we all have experiences while we sleep that we recognize as being more than just our unconscious musings. Our connection to these experiences comes through the *Sefirah Tiferet*.

Tiferet, in its highest manifestation, is the joining together of all opposing forces, the still-point after the ripple. In this way, it holds the truth of our essential nature within its depths. Thus, it is no accident that the Hebrew word for "truth" is *emet*, אמת. The first letter of the word *emet* is the first letter of the Hebrew alphabet, the *Aleph*, א. The last letter of the word *emet* is the last letter of the Hebrew alphabet, the *Tav*, ת, while the middle letter of *emet*, the *Mem*, מ, is in the exact middle of the Hebrew alphabet. This is meant to signify that it is only in the coming together and reconciliation of opposites that spiritual truth can be attained. During Sound Prayer we use the power inherent in the truth of *Tiferet* to align and center ourselves.

Netzah

Netzah (Eternity) is the *Sefirah* of Vision and of Prophecy. On *Adam Kadmon* it is visualized on the right hip, and it is associated with Moshe Rabbainu, also known as the prophet and teacher Moses. It was Moses whose vision and prophecy led the Israelites out of slavery in Egypt and brought them the Ten Commandments.

In the Biblical verse from which its name comes, the word *Netzah* can be translated as both "eternity" and "victory." It thus refers to both the timelessness of God's being and the triumph of His creation. *Netzah* is the ability to envision and the desire to build. It is reflective of our creative vision of the future and our earthly dreams as they relate to career, family, and worldly success. At its highest human level, *Netzah* is the ability to articulate eternal truths through prophecy.

Hod

Hod (Splendor) is visualized on the left hip of *Adam Kadmon*. Whereas *Netzah* is vision, *Hod* is actualization. *Hod* is associated with Aaron, Moses' brother, who was responsible for implementing Moses' vision and prophecy. Aaron served as Moses' spokesman, as it is written: "And you shall speak to Aaron and put words in his mouth, and I will be with your mouth and with his mouth. . . . Aaron will be your spokesman and you, Moses, will be unto him as a god."[13]

In its highest human form, *Hod* gives resplendent reality to *Netzah*'s timeless vision and prophecy, thereby manifesting the splendor of God's spiritual presence here on earth. On a more mundane level, it is our ability to materialize things in the physical world through such activities as politics, architecture, art, and childbearing.

The placement of *Netzah* on the right hip of *Adam Kadmon*, and *Hod* on the left hip, symbolizes that they are both required for us to "walk" forward. Vision without actualization is simply dreaming; action without vision is dry and sterile.

The word *Hod* is also related to the Hebrew word *hoddah*. One of *hoddah*'s meanings is "he acknowledged" and in this case the relationship points to the acknowledgement of a gift, the gift of vision bestowed upon *Hod* by *Netzah*, enabling it to carry out God's purpose on earth.

Yesod

Yesod (The All) is the earthly seat of sexual desire and a wellspring of vital power. Visualized in the genital area of *Adam Kadmon*, it is also the location through which new souls enter the world. *Yesod* therefore is a holy place, since the procreative power given to men and women is a direct function of God's own creative power.

Yesod is called the All because its primary function is to act as a funnel for the all-encompassing life force of creation after it cascades through the first eight *Sefirot* on its journey from the first *Sefirah*, *Keter*, to its final receptacle, the last *Sefirah*, *Malkhut*. In this way *Yesod* is the connector between heaven and earth, and is therefore also called "Foundation."

Yesod's function as the foundational *Sefirah* accounts for its association with righteousness. It is said that the world continues to exist only because, at any given moment, there are always thirty-six just human beings whose righteousness sustains it. While they themselves may be unaware of their role, if it were not for the righteousness of these thirty-six, the world would be destroyed because of its iniquity. Thus, it is said that the *Tzaddik,* or righteous one, is the "foundation of the world."[14]

This also accounts for *Yesod*'s association with the biblical character of Joseph. Joseph was a noble and righteous man whose character traits included loving kindness, compassion, and the wisdom to understand that the harsh challenges in his life were necessary for the fulfillment of God's divine plan.

Malkhut

Malkhut (Kingdom) is the receptacle for the gathered forces of *Yesod*. It is the *Sefirah* of the world of phenomena and earthly being, the physical palace of God. In its highest manifestation, it is the Creator's Presence, exhibiting itself to us as the female aspect known as the *Shekhinah*.

This is the aspect of God that discloses the possibility of grace and spiritual ascension. When we reach to God in Sound Prayer, it is the vibration and beauty of the *Shekhinah* that we experience.

Malkhut is the mirror of *Keter*, a place where the glory of the Creator, the purely spiritual and ineffable, is received and projected as the material manifestation of reality and then reflected back to *Keter* itself. While *Keter* sits above the head of *Adam Kadmon, Malkhut* lies just beneath the torso. If *Keter* is the light of creation, *Malkhut* is the wick to which the light-giving flame is attached. It is "the breath (that emanates) from breath,"[15] the final effect of the First Cause, God's created Kingdom.

Daat

Daat (Knowledge) is not counted among the *Sefirot*, yet it occupies a critical place on *Adam Kadmon* and plays an essential role in Sound Prayer (see figure 6.3).

Often called the non-Sefirah *Sefirah*, *Daat*'s location at the neck of *Adam Kadmon* is a clear indication of its importance. The neck is where God's spiritual force exerts its most persistent pressure as it attempts to make its way into our heart. This is why the *Zohar* refers to Jerusalem, which is considered the center of the spiritual world, and through which all spiritual power on earth flows, as "the neck of the Universe."[16] It is also why God, in his wrath, called the Israelites a "stiff necked people" when, after he delivered them from bondage in Egypt, they turned away from Him in the desert to worship the golden calf.[17]

The word *daat* derives from the same Biblical verse as the *Sefirot Keter*, *Hokhmah* and *Binah*: "I have filled him with the spirit of God, with wisdom, with understanding and with knowledge (*daat*) . . ."[18] In Hebrew, the word *daat* is also related to the word *yadah*, which means "he knew," as in the Biblical phrase "Adam knew H̲avah his wife."[19] Here the word "knew" refers to a knowing that arises not out of the intellect but rather out of intimacy and relatedness. In the case of *Daat*, its intimacy and relatedness to the *Sefirah Keter* allows *Daat* to perform its crucial function as the "exteriorization" of this exalted *Sefirah*.

Adam Kadmon: Primordial Man

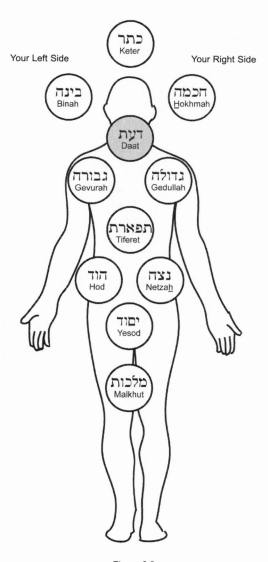

Figure 6:3

This "exteriorization" plays a fundamental role in Sound Prayer. Because of the crowning place that *Keter* occupies among the worlds, its sound may not be used in prayer. Yet there is need to draw on the power of *Keter* during our Sound Prayers. This is accomplished through the efficacy of *Daat*.

The placement of *Daat* at the throat of *Adam Kadmon* reflects that its power is directly related to our voice, which is the most spiritualized aspect of our physical being. The Biblical command not to speak the name of the Lord in vain relates to the importance of safeguarding the inherent power and holiness of *Daat* by maintaining the purity of our voice. The importance of keeping our voice pure is also one of the reasons behind the imperative not to speak ill of others.

Sound Prayer uses *Daat*'s special relationship to the *Sefirah Keter* to bring all of the other *Sefirot* together in balance and harmony. It is our voice, manifesting through *Daat* that creates the *tzinnorot*, or channels, that connect the *Sefirot* one to another.

7

Awakening

LIVING IN THE ORDINARY world with extraordinary consciousness is the reward of a spiritual life. My personal spiritual journey leaves no doubt in my mind as to the existence of a higher reality. It also leaves no doubt that each of us can live in its light, while still being part of this world.

When we awaken to this higher reality, we achieve the correct balance of all the *Sefirot* on *Adam Kadmon* and we reconnect with our true nature; we live with a deep sense of being fully present, and know in our heart that we are not alone. To truly possess this knowledge and to partake of this higher state of consciousness, however, we must stop clinging to the past, and leave behind our worry over the future. We cannot cross the frontier to this awakened state carrying the weight of all our old baggage.

During every lifetime, we have numerous opportunities to set down our burdens and to break away from our old worldview. Often these opportunities come during times of radical change in our circumstances when the underpinnings of our world, carefully constructed over the years, suddenly give way. Perhaps we come to find our work or our family life empty, or a dream to which we have dedicated our lives simply stops exerting its pull. Perhaps we experience a life-threatening illness, a break-up with a long-time partner, betrayal by a friend, or the loss of a cherished job.

Whatever the circumstances, these moments of crisis are also great opportunities. In the struggle to stay afloat, long-submerged thoughts, feelings, and desires of our soul arise.

In times of personal turmoil, when old rules no longer seem to apply, we are literally pushed back on ourselves. We feel grief and rage at the demise of the familiar and predictable world we relied on. Our sense of justice and order is violated. We are forced to confront the fragile nature of our support structures and the tenuous state of our belief systems. Our vulnerability becomes all too clear, bringing with it confusion, pain, and sorrow. In this disconnect between our old existence and the reality of our changed lives, there is real possibility for spiritual growth—there is the opportunity for our *neshamah*, our higher soul, to speak and be heard.

In these difficult moments, we have a choice. We can fight to recreate the past by simply returning to old patterns—we can cling to a destructive relationship; we can try to start a failed business over again, even though it gave us little satisfaction to begin with; we can allow grief to overtake us; we can give up dreaming altogether. The alternative is to go deeper into the well of our being to find a broader, more expansive, and more sustaining vision for ourselves.

The fires of our essential nature are never extinguished, only hidden, like embers in a smoldering fire. The challenge is to rekindle our fire, live fully in the present, leave the past behind, refocus our energy, and embark on a new path to find our true purpose and higher self. Those willing to dedicate themselves to this journey can find transformation beyond their greatest expectations.

In the face of these opportunities, we are often held back by our fear that we are not up to the task. In times of stress, our awareness of our imperfections and shortcomings is keen. Focused on our faults and vulnerabilities, we assume them to be insurmountable obstacles; we doubt our prospects, and memories of our mistakes haunt us.

During these times, we also need to battle the fear that by opening ourselves to a spiritual path, we will become unacceptable in the eyes of others. We may even be held back by the fear that in seeking a new path we will lose touch with reality. We fear that we will end up losing control, become vulnerable, naked and undefended, strangers in a strange land.

It is at these times that we must ask ourselves, "What do we owe other people? Do we owe them our essence? Do we serve others by reducing or extinguishing our personal flame?" The answer is that sustaining a false view of the world, in order to provide comfort to others about their own lives and choices, is neither good for them nor good for us.

At these crossroads in our lives, Sound Prayer is especially helpful. The practice of Sound Prayer can give us great support, as well as the will to move forward. It reminds us of the greater reality to which we are connected, and grounds us in our own inner strength. Because it speaks the language of the soul, as well as the language of creation, it reminds us of what we already know.

Over time, fear confronted becomes courage, and confusion gives way to clarity. Doubt is replaced with faith, and only uncertainty remains. But we learn to dance with uncertainty. When we act without expectation of reward, life retains its quality of surprise. By easing our grip on our expectations of the future, we relinquish our tight hold on the defining nature of the past.

In the process we learn a great lesson: the true nature of reality is such that there is no security, and that the outcome can never be assured. Circumstances are such that we have no other choice than to walk in faith. Having faith in our connection to God in the present moment, acting with passion to create a new future, is all that is needed. No longer desiring to know what cannot be known, giving up the need to know what is going to happen, we leave anxiety and fear behind. This is not an escape from reality; it is an embracing of Reality.

If we stay the distance, we will eventually notice that we have passed the point of no return. There is no way to get back to what was—it has lost its taste.

The slavery of the past, however, takes time to be exorcised, and we may often wonder if we can ever truly reach the Promised Land. We may need to spend a good deal of time in this desert, working on ourselves. The Jews of ancient times, having escaped slavery in Egypt, were required to spend forty years wandering in the desert. This was enough time for the generation brought up in slavery to die off, leaving their descendants who were born free of any slave mentality, to build a new nation.

A person seeking God and an end to the ego's tyranny must work continuously to achieve this goal, all the while acknowledging that the path is not a straight line. This process cannot take place overnight. Like a gardener, we must first uproot, then clear, enrich and aerate the soil to prepare the ground for a new planting. Our seeds first bear tender shoots and saplings that must be nurtured and protected. Not all will live, but ultimately, with careful tending, the necessary few will grow into strong plantings.

Once we accept that perfection is solely an attribute of God, we release ourselves from the self-defeating concept that failure to achieve our goals is always a sign of weakness.

To be strong means to be grounded. To be grounded means that our efforts at cultivating correct thought, speech, and action has led us to an accurate understanding of our strengths and weaknesses, as well as an honest appraisal of our own capacity for good and evil. From there, the path forward leads to surrender and freedom from fear.

It is at this time in particular that it is important to remember that ritual is in support of faith, not the other way around. When objects, rituals or ceremonies become talismans, when we believe that by themselves they are sufficient to protect us and bring us closer to God, they lose all reason for being.

In the end, we spin between the worlds—now angels, now human, now angels again. What we learn is very different from what we expect. In seeking to change ourselves, we become more like ourselves. Our work leads us to shed the old, worn-out garments of our false persona. We arrive at the gate of evolved consciousness as complete beings, having integrated our physical, emotional, intellectual, and spiritual nature. Naked, our essence is revealed, not only to ourselves, but for all the world to see.

Part Two

8

Sound Prayer

IN HEBREW, THE GRAMMAR of the verb "to pray"
(להתפלל) is reflexive, meaning that it describes an action
directed at oneself. This is recognition that, in its purest
form, prayer is something we do "to ourselves." It is an
attempt to raise ourselves to inner awareness and oneness with the Holy One. It is an act of pure longing to
build a space within for God to dwell; it is a cry of the
heart to serve as an offering to open the heavens.

This is the mystical teaching behind God's command
to Moses: "Speak to the Israelites and have them bring
Me an offering. Take the offering from those who give
because their hearts prompt them to do so. . . . And
they shall make Me a sanctuary, and I will live in their
midst."[1] The sanctuary referred to here is not just one
of wood, stone and mortar, but also the temple that we
can each build within ourselves.

In prayer, our higher soul, the *neshamah*, does not ask for assistance, but rather trembles with overwhelming love and yearning before God, offering itself as a receptacle into which the spirit of the Holy One may be poured. In this way we obey the command to "love your God with all your heart, with all your soul and with all your might."[2]

In contrast, when the *nefesh* or animal soul approaches God, it prays for its own well-being. It seeks to make bargains and offers trades. It agrees to be obedient in exchange for things like success, position, and wealth. Even when we get what we ask for, these prayers rarely satisfy our need to be heard. The absence of an answer, however, is also an answer.

At the level of our animal soul, deceived by our senses as to the nature of reality and smothered by the dense and coarse matter of the physical world, we think of ourselves as separate and apart from one another and the world around us. Sound Prayer takes us beyond this world. Just as the language of our *neshamah*, our higher soul, is not that of words or the duality of the everyday world they describe, so it is with Sound Prayer. The language of Sound Prayer is pure vibration. Using our voice to create sacred chants, our Sound Prayers take us beyond the language of our animal soul and offer us the opportunity to begin to taste the fruit of the Tree of Life.

Recall that, while the roots of the Tree of Life are in the heavens and its fruits are in our world, this tree also exists in reverse, with its roots in this world and its branches above. The trunk of this tree is like the spine of the universe, containing the nerves and impulses of an entire living, conscious organism. We can either nourish the branches of this tree through love of God and proper thought and behavior, or poison its fruit through hatred, base thoughts, and evil actions. Thus, each of us has the power to directly influence the highest forces in the upper worlds and therefore events here on earth. Sound Prayer offers us a sacred way to exercise this power for the good.

Our Sound Prayers send vibrations up the spinal column of all the worlds, shaking the spheres. In this way, we help bring our earthly world into alignment with the upper worlds as we attune to the rest of the universe. Sound Prayer promotes stability, integration, and peace in all the worlds by helping harmonize the many disparate forces within us and within the universe.

The *Kabbalah* teaches that the universe consists of four worlds. Our own world is called *Olam haAssiyah*, or the World of Making. The world immediately above ours is the world of the angels called *Olam haYetzirah*, or the World of Formation. Next is the World of Creation, called *Olam haBeriah*, followed by *Olam haAtzilut*, the World of Emanation.

Although most are only conscious of their existence in the everyday world of *Olam haAssiyah*, each of us has an intimate connection to all four worlds through our soul, which inhabits each of these worlds at all times. Each of us is a microcosm of the universe, and everything done to realign ourselves also helps realign the worlds.

When we refer to the "upper worlds," this is simply a metaphor. Each of the four worlds is embedded in the others. This is another meaning of the teaching that "The end is embedded in the beginning and the beginning in the end, like a flame in a burning coal."[3] Sound Prayer offers a connection to all the worlds, not as abstraction but in reality.

Experience during Sound Prayer teaches us that while our knowledge is finite, our consciousness is limitless. During Sound Prayer our individual fears and preoccupations melt away. Released from mundane concerns, we can align with the highest forces and come into a state of grace. Over time, as we approach the Holy One, our true nature becomes clearer, our soul's purpose emerges, and we rest in the All.

Sound Prayer is based on the fundamental truth that vibration is the elemental essence of all manifest being. The vibrations of our voice in Sound Prayer dedicated to God, and carried on the wings of our breath, reach out directly to the *Shekhinah*, God's female presence on earth. In so doing, we help unite what is separated and restore equilibrium to that which is out of balance. For, when we pray, it is as if we are clothing the *Shekhinah* with our prayer.

The power of our Sound Prayers lies in the fact that, far from being an echo of the sacred sounds used by

God in the creation, we are each part of those original vibrations. This is why sound in general, and chanting in particular, touches us so deeply. By focusing our *kavanah*, or intention, on various *Sefirot* while we pray with sound, we create vibrations that pluck the chords of all the worlds, resonate with the spheres, and bind ourselves to the highest roots. In this way, we each play a role in the universe's continuous becoming. Through Sound Prayer we return to the eternal now. Finding our way home, deep in the hidden recesses of our soul, we make our way to a place of transformational communion with *YHVH*, the Holy One.

The sacred sounds we make with our voices during Sound Prayer, combined with concentration on specific *Sefirot*, enable us to enter meditative states that bring us into an intimate relationship with God. This relationship unites body and soul, heaven and earth, male and female, thereby performing the vital spiritual function of reconciling all differences.

It is not surprising that the sound of our voice has such spiritual power, for the universe itself was created by sound. The *Zohar*'s description of the creation of the universe through sound is sheer poetry, beautiful and deeply mystical:

> At the outset the decision of the King made a tracing in the supernal effulgence, a lamp of scintillation, and there issued within the impenetrable recesses of the mysterious limitless a shapeless nucleus enclosed in a

ring, neither white nor black nor red nor green nor
any color at all. When he took measurements, he fash-
ioned colors to show within, and within the lamp
there issued a certain effluence from which colors were
imprinted below. . . .

The most mysterious Power enshrouded in the limitless clave, as it were, without cleaving its void,
remaining wholly unknowable until from the force of
the strokes there shone forth a supernal and mysterious point. Beyond that point there is no knowable,
and therefore it is called *Reishit* (beginning), the creative utterance which is the starting point of all.

. . . The Most Mysterious struck its void and
caused this point to shine. This "beginning" then
extended and made for itself a palace for its honor and
glory. There it sowed a sacred seed, which was to generate for the benefit of the universe . . . it sowed a seed
for its glory, just as the silkworm encloses itself, as it
were, in the palace of its own production which is
both useful and beautiful.

Thus by means of this "beginning" the Mysterious
Unknown made this palace. This palace is called
Elohim and this doctrine is contained in the words,
"By means of a beginning (it) created *Elohim*." The
Zohar [splendor] is that from which were created all
the creative utterances through the extension of the
point of this mysterious brightness.

. . . What is this seed? It consists of the graven letters, the secret source of the *Torah*, which issued from

the first point. That point sowed in the palace certain three vowel-points, *holam*, *shuruk* and *hirik*, which combined with one another and formed one entity, to wit, the Voice which issued through their union.[4]

The *Sefer Yetzirah* also teaches that sound was God's initial creative force. It states that *Keter*, the *Sefirah* directly associated with the initial act of creation, is "the Breath of the Living God" and goes on to speak of the mysteries of the sequence of creation as: "Voice and breath and speech. . . ."[5]

The Hebrew word translated here as "voice" is *kol*, which means "inarticulate sound." The *Sefer Yetzirah* thus makes the point that before speech, before God spoke the first "words" of creation: "Let there be light,"[6] it was *kol*, God's pure, non-verbal sounds, that began the process of creation.

This explains why Genesis, the first book of the Hebrew Bible, describes the process of creation as having two distinct parts. It begins by stating: "In the beginning God created the heaven and the earth . . . and the breath of God hovered on the face of the water."[7] Only then does Genesis go on to describe individual acts of creation brought about by God's spoken words, beginning with the utterance "Let there be light."

The power of sound is also highlighted in one of the more paradoxical phrases from the Hebrew Bible: "And all the people saw the sounds,"[8] which describes the experience of the Hebrews as God spoke the Ten

Commandments at Mount Sinai. The paradox of "seeing" sound is resolved when we understand that not only words, but sound itself, has the power to awaken our higher soul, thus changing the way we "see" things.

The Biblical story of Israel's priests using the vibrations produced by blowing upon a ram's horn or *Shofar* to bring down the walls of Jericho is yet another allusion to the power of sound. Even today, the blowing of the *Shofar* during prayer is meant to open the gates to heaven so that prayers can be received.

Still another indication of the power of sound lies in the fact that *Bereshit*, the first word of the Bible, usually translated as "In the beginning," can also be read in the Hebrew as "He created six."[9] This is a reference to the multidirectional nature of sound, which travels in six directions outward in a spherical wave, side to side, front to back, upwards and downwards from its source.

Sound is pure vibration, and vibration is the fundamental constituent of the universe. Everything vibrates, and the universe can be likened to a single string on an instrument, a string that generates an infinite number of different vibrational tones depending on the placement of God's bow.

The fact that the sacred sounds we make during Sound Prayer are created by our breath rather than in some other way is significant. Breath is life itself, God's great gift to us. The absence of breath marks the return of the body to dust and the return of our soul to God.

The sacredness of our breath is made clear in the Bible, which tells us that Adam lives because God "breathed into his nostrils the breath of life."[10]

The sacredness of breath is also why the Bible often likens God's Presence to wind, since the Hebrew word for wind, which is *ruah,* also means breath. The sacred connection between breath and life is also the reason that in Hebrew the word for the higher soul, *neshamah*, has the same root as the word *neshimah*, which also means breath.

From a mystical standpoint, every time we breathe out, a part of our essence is exhaled and momentarily rejoins with the universe. Then, each time we inhale, we take in God's essence. In this way, our soul is constantly in touch with the Divine and continually infused with God's spirit. This is why the simple act of breathing in and out can serve as a sacred reminder of God's Presence.

Yet, because breathing is mostly an unconscious act, it is easy to ignore the supernal wisdom that it imparts. Sound Prayer focuses our attention on our breath as it uses the sacred vibrations of our voices to reach out to God. In Sound Prayer our body, the repository of our soul, becomes a beautiful resonating chamber, an instrument for the soul's expression through our voice.

In addition to the vibrations we make with our voice during Sound Prayer, what exists between our sounds and the silence that follows is also sacred. In between sound and silence lies mystery and profundity—that which cannot be apprehended by our ordinary intellect or senses. Nevertheless it is real. During deep meditation in Sound Prayer it is possible to find the gateway to the mysteries of the other worlds—for the entrance to the subtle worlds can be found in the space between silence and sound, in the time between swiftness and pause, in the blank space, where everything comes momentarily to rest. This is what the prophet Elijah experienced when he heard *kol dmamah*, or the "voice of silence" just before he heard the voice of God.[11]

The prophet Ezekiel also experienced that which exists between silence and sound in his *Merkavah* or Chariot vision.[12] In this vision, Ezekiel describes the appearance of the *hashmal* at the threshold of the doorway to the other worlds. The meaning of the word *hashmal* is something scholars and mystics have puzzled over for centuries as it combines two sets of contradictory meanings.

Moses Maimonides, the great twelfth century scholar, divides the word *hashmal* into its two syllables: *hash*, which relates to swiftness, and *mal*, which relates to pause. He then makes the point that *hash* is related to the Hebrew word heheshethi or "I became silent," a phrase found in Isaiah,[13] while *mal* is directly related to speech itself. Thus *hashmal* is "speaking silence."[14]

In this way, the *hashmal* embodies the logical contradiction inherent in the four distinct Kabbalistic worlds being embedded in each other, occupying the same space and time. While experience of the *hashmal* is given only to the most gifted of visionaries and prophets, we can begin to appreciate its possibilities during the meditative states that we can enter during Sound Prayer.

Sound Prayer rests on four cornerstones. The first and most important is our *dvekut,* or our devotion to cling to God. In this regard, when standing before the Holy One, neither skill, possessions, nor accomplishment count. Before the One to whom we cannot lie, only the naked yearning of our heart matters. Only our sincere inner cry and our heart's deepest longing has sufficient power to pierce the veil that separates us from the upper worlds, and to build a fitting sanctuary within us for God to dwell.

Our *dvekut* arises from the depths of our being where we fully understand the suffering that occurs when we are separated and apart from God. The painfulness of separation from the Holy One is why, in the Bible, the description of the second day of creation differs from all the rest. It is the day when God separated heaven from earth, and it is the only day in the creation story where it is not written: "God saw that it was good."[15]

The second cornerstone of Sound Prayer is our intention or *kavanah* during our prayers themselves. Once we have offered up our heart to God, our *kavanah* or intention during Sound Prayer focuses on cultivating channels between specific *Sefirot* on the Tree of Life. This brings the opposing and competing aspects of the

Sefirot into harmony, both within ourselves and in the worlds. The Hebrew word *kavanah* is related to the word *kivun*, or direction, and it is our *kavanah* that gives direction to our prayer.

The channels created by our Sound Prayers are called *tzinnorot*, and on a personal level they promote internal alignment and integration, leading step-by-step to the awakening of our higher soul.

Within creation itself, our Sound Prayers help balance the forces of the universe, bringing healing in an act of *Tikkun Olam* or "repair of the world." According to the *Kabbalah*, it is a uniquely human responsibility to counteract forces of darkness, separation, and destruction. Sound Prayer can help us fulfill this obligation.

While it is difficult to be fully human and to reconcile our intellectual, emotional, and physical natures, every aspect of our being must participate in order to attain higher levels of consciousness. Therefore, the practice of Sound Prayer starts by creating channels between three different pairs of *Sefirot*: *Hokhmah* (Wisdom) and *Binah* (Understanding), *Gedullah* (Love) and *Gevurah* (Judgement), and *Netzah* (Vision) and *Hod* (Manifestation).

These channels are of the utmost importance in our daily lives. They reflect these truths: Without wisdom, our understanding is like a blunt instrument and without understanding, wisdom is speechless. Love without the discrimination of judgement is a recipe for disaster, while judgement untempered by love and mercy is senseless cruelty. Manifestation without vision is bloodless and shallow, yet vision without manifestation is but an empty dream.

The third foundation stone of Sound Prayer is sound itself. The sacredness of the specific sounds we use in Sound Prayer and the power of their vibration derive from their connection to the initial act of creation. Each sound is related to a particular *Sefirah*, and each has its own unique role in prayer.

The fourth component of Sound Prayer relates to our connection with *Olam haYetzirah*, the world of the angels. We are often confused about the nature of the spiritual. Although it is true that we must act as if we are solely responsible for our soul's spiritual growth, it is a mistake to think that we can accomplish the task of being fully human by ourselves.

Although much depends on our own resolve, the beings and forces of the upper worlds, especially the angels, are important in getting our prayers to their destination, and in the success of our soul's journey. This is what is meant when it is said that we must act as if everything depends on ourselves and pray as if everything depends on God.

The thirteenth century Kabbalist Joseph Gikatila, commenting on Psalm ninety-one, explained these matters by teaching that there are many beings living in the heavens and here on earth, and before our prayers ascend to heaven they must pass among them. Some of these beings are of a destructive nature, intent on robbing our prayers of their power. Speaking of the individual in prayer, Gikatila writes: "One who walks on the roads between heaven and earth is in a place of danger. . . . If the supplicant has merit the prayer will find its way, but if there is no merit, the prayer will be at the mercy of thieves and powerful destructive forces which can prevent or delay the prayer from ascending."[16] The *Sefer haZohar* makes the same point when it says: "If the prayer is not whole, harmful angels will run after it."[17]

Being held worthy and righteous before God is something we must always strive for, since "God delights in the prayers of the righteous."[18] However, becoming worthy is a process. If we wait for our own perfection, we will never pray. So our prayers need assistance along the way. When our prayers are made with pure intention and the genuine yearning of our heart, the help they need comes from the world of the angels.

In Sound Prayer we are like an archer: yearning is our bow, and our intention, or *kavanah*, is our bowstring. Our arrows are the sounds we use, and it is upon the wings of the angels that our arrows take flight to the Lord our God.

9

The Sacred Sounds
of the Sefirot

THE SOUNDS WE MAKE with our breath in Sound Prayer are very specific. They are the sounds associated with creation itself, which are the Hebrew vowel sounds represented in the Hebrew language by symbols called vowel points or *nekudot*.

Both the *Zohar* and the *Bahir* speak of the power of the *nekudot*. The *Zohar* refers to the letters of the Hebrew alphabet as "the body" and the vowel points as their "animating spirit."[1] The *Bahir* states that the vowel points are related "to the letters in the same manner as the soul to the human body" and goes on to point out that "Human beings cannot exist without a soul, and one cannot say anything without the vowel points."[2] The *Bahir* also acknowledges the gift of life in the vowel points when it states that: "The letters endure through the vowel points, which animate them."[3]

The sacred nature of the Hebrew vowel points is also referred to in Ezekiel's vision of two types of angels, wherein it is written: "for the spirit of the *Hayah* was in the *Ophanim*."[4] The coordinated movements of these two types of angels, the *Hayah* and the *Ophanim*, are akin to the movement of our soul with our body, just like the movement of the sacred vowel points with the Hebrew letters.

Each *Sefirah* has a specific vowel sound that belongs to it (see figures 9:1 and 9:2).[5] The vowel sound that belongs to a particular *Sefirah* is determined by many things, including:

- sources in *Kabbalah* that associate the names of the vowel points with specific qualities, which in turn link them to specific *Sefirot*;
- the particular part of our body that the sound resonates with, which can then be correlated with the associated *Sefirah*;
- the shape of the symbols used to represent the sounds, which themselves divulge meaning;
- hidden references found in Ezekiel's *Merkavah*, or Chariot vision;
- the teachings of answering angels.

The sounds of the *Sefirot*, and the power inherent in them must be used with great care and humility. Since

The Tree of Life

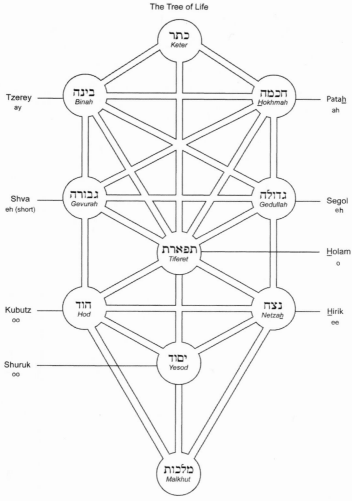

Keter — כתר
Keter

בינה — Binah
Binah

חכמה — Hokhmah
Hokhmah

Tzerey
ay

Pataḥ
ah

גבורה
Gevurah

גדולה
Gedullah

Shva
eh (short)

Segol
eh

תפארת
Tiferet

Holam
o

הוד
Hod

נצח
Netzaḥ

Kubutz
oo

Hirik
ee

יסוד
Yesod

Shuruk
oo

מלכות
Malkhut

Figure 9:1

The Vowel Sounds of the *Sefirot*

Vowel Name	Symbol	Sound	As In	Placement	Sefirah
Kamatz	⊤	aw	raw	bottom	Keter
Patah	▬	ah	rah	bottom	Hokhmah
Tzerey	• •	ay	say	bottom	Binah
Segol	•.•	eh	wet	bottom	Gedullah
Shva	⦂	silent or eh (short)	eh	bottom	Gevurah
Holam	•	o	oh	upper left	Tiferet
Hirik	•	ee	see	bottom	Netzah
Kubutz	•.•	oo	too	bottom	Hod
Shuruk	•	oo	too	center left of letter Vav	Yesod
No Vowel					Malkhut

Figure 9.2

their use in Sound Prayer offers the possibility of entering into the Divine Presence, our intention and concentration in the moment of prayer must be based on love.

The Sounds of the *Sefirot*:

Keter (The Crown)
The sound for *Keter*, symbolized by the *Kamatz* is the
sound for directly approaching the Godhead. It is not
used in Sound Prayer.

Hokhmah (Wisdom)

The sound for <u>H</u>okhmah is "ah" as in "rah." The Hebrew name for this vowel sound is *pata<u>h</u>* and its symbol is a straight horizontal line. It is the line of simultaneous revelation and concealment. It must be concentrated upon to yield its secret, for a straight line, in its simplicity, appears to have none.

The word *pata<u>h</u>* means an opening. The *pata<u>h</u>* stands for the opening to the other worlds and the inherent spiritual wisdom that resides at all times within our *neshamah*, our higher soul. As a gateway to the Divine, it is related to Psalm twenty-four: "Open the gates (*pit<u>h</u>ey*) of the world and the King of Glory will come."[6]

Binah (Understanding)

The sound for *Binah* is "ay" as in "say." Its symbol is the *tzerey*. *Binah* is where God sits on an "exalted Throne"[7] lowering Himself so that He can be reached. The two horizontal points of the *tzerey* represent the two places upon which our feet must stand in order to reach God's throne and gain understanding

Gedullah (Greatness and Unconditional Love)

The sound for *Gedullah* is "eh" as in "wet." This vowel sound is called the *segol* and it is symbolized by three points in the pattern of an inverted triangle, two above and one below, pointing to the distinction between the upper and lower worlds. The *Sefirah Gedullah* receives its precious unconditional love from the upper worlds, sending it on to the lower realms. As the *Tikkuney haZohar* relates: "The three dots are likened to three precious stones which are the three patriarchs."[8]

The precious nature of unconditional love is also reflected in the fact that the word *segol* is related to the word *segullah* or "treasure." As it is written: "What is the meaning of the *segol*? Its name is *Segullah*."[9]

Gevurah (Strength and Strict Judgement)

The sound for *Gevurah* is the *shva*, and it is the hard, unyielding short sound of "eh."[10] The *shva* is symbolized by two points, one directly below the other. It has as its root the Hebrew word *shva*, which comes from the story of Job. It was the men from the land of *Shva* who inflicted harsh judgement on Job and his family.[11]

The *shva* is the sound for strength that overpowers, yet as the great Kabbalist Rabbi Joseph Gikatila tells us: "The *shva* cannot stand on its own. . . . It always appears with other vowels. . . . It is rather like the moon which shines because it reflects the sun."[12] Thus, we are taught that in holy matters, mere strength is never sufficient.

Tiferet (Beauty and Harmony)

The sound for *Tiferet* is the *holam* and it is the rounded sound of "o" as in the word "oh." Its symbol is a single point located at the upper left of a letter and, according to the *Bahir*, it is the sound most associated with the soul itself.

In Hebrew, the vowel point *holam* most often

accompanies the letter *Vav*, and *vav* itself is a word that means hook. The solar plexus, where *Tiferet* is located, is the place where the soul hooks to the body and from which an aspect of our soul departs during sleep to fly to God for instruction.

The Hebrew word for dream (*ḥalom*) is related to the vowel sound *ḥolam*, and as Rabbi Gikatila teaches: "All light and goodness depend on the *ḥolam*,"[13] since in the dream state we have the opportunity to reach beyond our physical life and see a road to the spiritual. Dreams take us to another world where we can find the pathway out of the constricting life of the *nefesh*, through the medium of the *ruaḥ*.

The word *ḥolam* is also related to the word *aḥlama* which is the Hebrew word for the gem amethyst. This points to the beauty which is *Tiferet*.

In addition, the word *ḥolam* is related to the word *ḥolayim*, which means "diseases." Their relationship is explained by the *Bahir* in response to a question as to the nature of the *ḥolam*. The *Bahir* tells us that *ḥolam* represents the *neshamah* or higher soul and, "If you listen to your *neshamah*, your body will heal in the future to come, but if you rebel against your *neshamah* the consequences will be mental sickness, which in turn will bring disease."[14]

Netzah (Eternity and Victory)
Netzaḥ represents the permanence and vision of God's power as it manifests and materializes in the universe.

The sound for *Netzah* is the *hirik* pronounced "ee" as in "see." Its symbol is a single point at the bottom of a letter. The *Bahir* compares the permanence of *Netzah* to ice, the hardened state of water, and the word "*hirik*" (חיריק) contains the same letters as the Hebrew word for "ice" (קרח).[15]

The *Zohar* also points to a connection between ice, and the sound of the *hirik*, as well as the visionary aspect of *Netzah*. In Ezekiel's vision of the Chariot, the angels who accompany the chariot each have an "awesome ice canopy" above their heads, a phenomenon that reflects the power of God.[16] The *Sefer haZohar* tells us that this ice of the north melts when it comes into contact with the warmth of the south to which it is drawn.[17] The resulting river of water flows willingly, bringing the visionary forces of the spiritual world to nourish the physical.

Hod (Splendor)

The sound for *Hod* is the *kubutz*, which is pronounced "oo" as in "too." It is symbolized by three points on a slant from left to right. The three points of the *kubutz* are like three steps that lead from *Netzah* (Eternity) to *Yesod*, the foundational *Sefirah* upon which the ladder rests.

Yesod (Foundation and the All)

The sound for *Yesod* is the *shuruk* and is pronounced "oo" as in "too" in the same manner as the sound for

Hod.[18] Its symbol is a single point located in the center left of the letter *vav*. In Hebrew through a simple rearrangement of the letters, the word *shuruk* transforms into the word *kesher*, which means "tie." *Shuruk* ties all things together. Upon its foundation the world and its fate rest and "all of redemption hangs upon the *shuruk*."[19]

Malkhut (Kingdom)

Malkhut does not have a vowel sound. Instead it receives the vibrations of *Yesod* and returns those vibrations in circular fashion back to *Keter*. This is yet another meaning that follows from the teaching in the *Sefer Yetzirah* that "the end is embedded in the beginning, and the beginning in the end, as a flame in a burning coal."[20]

10

Sound Prayer Instruction

Preparation for Sound Prayer:
Begin by preparing yourself for entering a holy space. The concept of separation between the sacred and the profane, the pure and the impure, is an important one. When we approach an earthly king, we accord him great honor, and would not seek an audience without proper preparation. As Holy Scripture admonishes, "One cannot approach a King wearing a sack cloth."[1] To approach the heavenly King, it is that much more imperative that we cleanse both our outer and inner self as best we can.

It is best to choose a special place in your home to designate for prayer and meditation, one that you can use on a daily basis. Keep this special place as clean as possible. If there is a bathroom attached, make sure the door is closed before beginning your Sound Prayers.

Wear comfortable clothes in order to allow your breath to move easily through your body. Sit up straight, on either a chair or a cushion. If on a chair, do not cross your legs, and make sure that your feet are touching the floor. If you use a cushion, sit in a comfortable posture. In either case sit with your spinal column erect, your shoulders at ease and your body relaxed.

Think of your body as a physical instrument, a resonating chamber, and imagine your organs and bones about to resonate with your voice. Keeping your shoulders relaxed, allow your hands to rest easily in your lap. To help your posture, gently tighten the muscles of the abdomen and let your neck float free. To keep external distractions to a minimum you may close your eyes. The quieter you can be internally before beginning, the better.

Begin by saying a brief prayer in recognition of the One. Use whatever words come to your mind, but always end with words of thanks. Since we are dealing with the sacred, as we approach God through the gates that uphold the universe, our heart's intention must be pure and uncorrupted by thoughts of material gain. Equally important, we must be free of negative emotions such as anger, jealousy, and hatred. Remember to be humble and respectful, neither self-critical, nor inflated with self-importance.

When offering Sound Prayers, let your sounds be effortless and gentle, and make each sound only as long as your breath lasts. Do not strain, as it will constrain your breath, and tighten your voice. Remember that you must approach the King through surrender, not through effort. Keep in mind that it is not important to have a good voice or to be able to sing on key. Sound Prayer is not performance—it is a reaching out to God, to whom we are completely transparent.

If praying in a group, do not attempt to harmonize or to copy the length or pitch of anyone else's sounds. In the same way as two pendulums moving at different rates will synchronize when placed near each other, your individual voices raised to express your own soul's song will naturally, without effort, produce a beautiful symphony.

Most important, remember that in Sound Prayer, your sounds do not have power in and of themselves. They must be made with *kavanah*, or intention, in order to reach their mark. It is only through *kavanah* that your sounds can become a means of communication and connection to God. Every human being possesses the possibility of this connection, but only when our hearts and minds are focused with correct intention do our sounds have force. The *Sefirot* are gates of communication with God, but they must be used properly.

Keep in mind that to play an instrument well we must first learn technique and form; but to play sublimely we must leave technique behind and become one with our music. Becoming one with our sounds is an important part of Sound Prayer.

The four Sound Prayers that follow are:

COMPASSION
INTEGRATION
HEALING
ALIGNMENT

Each of these Sound Prayers can be done individually or they can be done one after another in the order given. Each one is anchored by the components of the Central Column of the Tree of Life, specifically the *Sefirot Tiferet* and *Yesod*. In addition, several of these Sound Prayers make use of our heart center (see figure 10:1) and each one utilizes the integrative power of *Daat*, which comes through the voice itself.

The Central Column is the trunk of the Tree of Life. The trunk of this tree has its feet firmly planted in the ground while its topmost portion reaches toward the heavens. Like the trunk of any tree, this column is a place of great stability and strength. It is from such a place that we can most easily access the higher realms.

Under certain circumstances, the six *Sefirot* that lie outside the Central Column can also be used as the anchor of Sound Prayers. However, these prayers must be made under careful supervision, since their improper use can bring about physical and emotional imbalances.

Please read the set of instructions for each Sound Prayer in its entirety before beginning.

Central Column

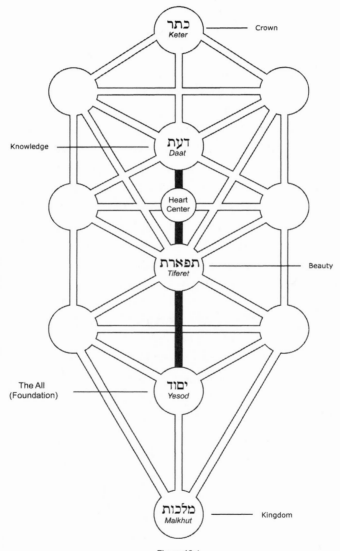

כתר
Keter
Crown

דעת
Daat
Knowledge

Heart
Center

תפארת
Tiferet
Beauty

יסוד
Yesod
The All
(Foundation)

מלכות
Malkhut
Kingdom

Figure 10:1

COMPASSION

. . .

In this Sound Prayer we use the sound of <u>H</u>okhmah, or "wisdom consciousness," for it is a wise person that knows compassion, and without compassion there can be no peace. This sound is "AH" as in "rah." It is the sound of the Hebrew vowel *pata<u>h</u>*.

Our anchor in this prayer is the *Sefirah Tiferet*, the *Sefirah* of beauty, peace, and harmony. In the Kabbalistic universe, compassion results from the tempering of strict judgement, in the form of the *Sefirah Gevurah*, with its opposite, *Gedullah*, the *Sefirah* of unconditional love. Thus, true compassion results not from abandoning judgement but rather from its transformation.

- Close your eyes and observe one or two minutes of silence. Concentrate on the inhalations and exhalations of your breath as you relax your body. Without holding your breath or prolonging your exhalation, allow yourself to become aware of the "space" between breathing in and out.

- Keeping your eyes closed, visualize the sacred sounds you are about to make as the vibrations of a great string. This string, called "The Great Octave" is anchored at each end by the two *Sefirot*, *Keter* and *Malkhut*, and contains eight sparks of light, which represent the remaining eight *Sefirot* (see figure 10:2). Spend a minute or two imagining the sounds you are about to make resonating through these eight separate sparks.

- Now, with your eyes still closed, visualize an inverted triangle on your body (see figure 10:3). The two top points are just below the level of each shoulder. The point under your left shoulder represents the *Sefirah* of strict judgement, *Gevurah*, and the opposite point represents the *Sefirah* of unconditional love, *Gedullah*. The lower point of this triangle is located at the solar plexus, which is just beneath the rib cage, above your waist. This is where *Tiferet*, the *Sefirah* of peace, beauty, and harmony, is located. Spend a few minutes making this triangle as real as you can in your mind's eye. As with all Sound Prayers, it is not necessary to remember which *Sefirah* belongs to which point on the triangle you are visualizing, or what any given *Sefirah* represents. Your sounds will do this for you. You simply need to visualize the triangle itself.

- Keeping your eyes closed, turn your total attention to *Tiferet* at the bottom point of the triangle at your solar plexus.

- Now, make the sound of "AH" three times, sending the sound effortlessly through *Tiferet* at the solar plexus. Your focus should be to generate

The Great Octave

Figure 10:2

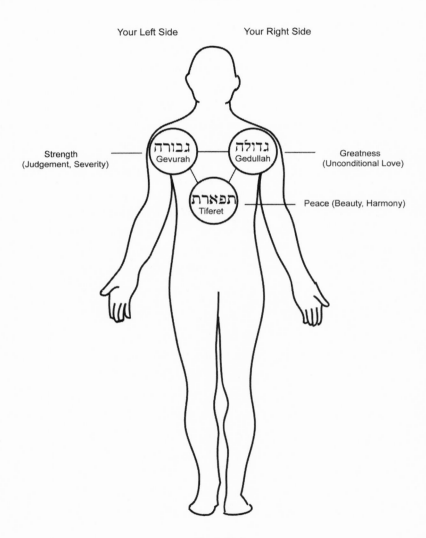

Figure 10:3

compassion for yourself. By intending to send your sound through your solar plexus, as if it were your mouth, you will automatically find the right pitch. Make each "AH" sound for only as long as it seems natural. As you make each sound, remember to keep your intention focused on generating compassion for yourself. We cannot experience compassion for others unless we are compassionate to ourselves.

- Now, once again visualize the same inverted triangle, as if it were drawn directly on your body, and then return your attention to your solar plexus. Make another three "AH" sounds, still directing them through your solar plexus. This time keep your focus on generating compassion toward a specific individual or group you know to be suffering.

- Again, after refocusing on the three corners of the inverted triangle, bring your attention back to your solar plexus and make another three "AH" sounds. Continue to think of your sounds as coming from your solar plexus, but this time keep your intention directed toward generating compassion toward an individual or group that is personally causing you difficulty. You may notice that with this intention in mind, your "AH" sound will have a different tone. This is not unusual and will not detract from the power of the prayer.

- Once more, after refocusing on each corner of the triangle, make three "AH" sounds through your solar plexus. This time, keep your focus on generating compassion toward all living beings, as well as the universe itself, in order that we may heal from all division.

- Finish your Sound Prayer by once more refocusing on each corner of the inverted triangle, and then making one long "AH" sound through your solar plexus, keeping focused once again on generating compassion toward yourself.

- Over time, you should increase the number of sounds that you make during each of the five parts of this prayer. Eventually you should make this prayer repeating the sound of "AH" a total of twenty-six times. We use twenty-six sounds because twenty-six is the numerical equivalent of the four-letter unpronounceable name of God, *YHVH*. Make six sounds of "AH" during the first four parts and end by making a long sound of "AH" twice.

INTEGRATION

. . .

In this Sound Prayer we use the sound of the vowel point *ḥolam*, the rounded sound of "O" as in "oh." Our intention in this prayer is to generate peace and harmony by creating channels, or *tzinnorot*, between seven different *Sefirot* (see figure 10:4).

Genuine peace and harmony are achieved in the reconciliation of opposites. We come to peace when we do not attempt to prevail over warring elements within ourselves or over others, but rather regard all conflict as different aspects of the One. Since we are only human, this is a state of mind that few can maintain for long periods. Even achieving this state for short lengths of time, however, has great restorative powers.

This is an excellent prayer to do before going to sleep at night.

- Close your eyes and observe one or two minutes of silence. Concentrate on the inhalations and exhalations of your breath as you continue to relax your body. Without holding your breath or prolonging your exhalation, allow yourself to be aware of the "space" between breathing in and out.

Integration

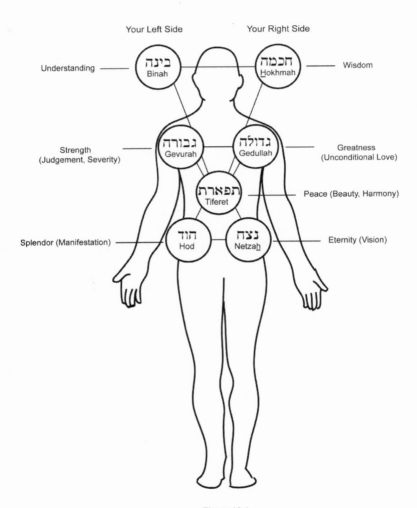

Your Left Side   Your Right Side

Understanding ——— בינה   חכמה ——— Wisdom
                      Binah   Hokhmah

Strength ———   גבורה   גדולה   ——— Greatness
(Judgement, Severity) Gevurah   Gedullah   (Unconditional Love)

                      תפארת
                      Tiferet   ——— Peace (Beauty, Harmony)

Splendor (Manifestation) ——— הוד   נצח   ——— Eternity (Vision)
                              Hod   Netzah

Figure 10:4

- Begin by focusing on your solar plexus at the center of your body, above the waist and below the rib cage.

- Now make the rounded sound of "O" three times with the intention to send the sound effortlessly through the solar plexus and out into the space around you. Think of yourself as generating peace through all the worlds.

- Next, imagine a triangle whose top point, the *Sefirah Tiferet*, is located at your solar plexus, and whose other two points are the *Sefirah Hod* at the left hip and the *Sefirah Netzah* at the right hip (see figure 10:5). In this prayer, *Hod* represents actualization and *Netzah* represents vision. Keep in mind, it is not necessary to remember which *Sefirah* belongs to which point on the triangle you are visualizing, nor what any given *Sefirah* represents. You simply need to visualize the triangle itself.

- Now, make three rounded "O" sounds. Send the sound effortlessly through the solar plexus while imagining the sound drifting downward from your solar plexus, gently, without strain or effort, flowing through the area around your left and right hip simultaneously. In this way, maintain a clear intention to connect your solar plexus with these two areas.

Integration

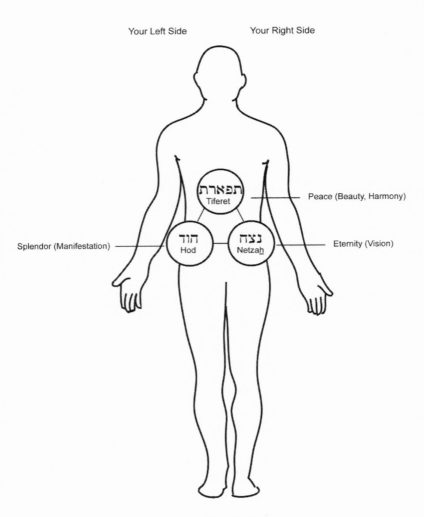

Your Left Side   Your Right Side

תפארת
Tiferet

Peace (Beauty, Harmony)

הוד
Hod

Splendor (Manifestation)

נצח
Netzah

Eternity (Vision)

Figure 10:5

- Now, visualize an inverted triangle similar to the one you used in the first Sound Prayer. Once again, the lowest point of this triangle is located at the solar plexus, which is just beneath the rib cage above your waist. The other two points are just below the level of each shoulder. The left corner is the *Sefirah Gevurah* representing judgement and severity. At the right corner is the *Sefirah Gedullah* representing unconditional love (see figure 10:6). With eyes closed, spend time making this triangle as real as you can in your mind's eye. Remember that you only need to visualize the triangle. There is no need to keep the *Sefirot* in mind.

- Now, make three rounded "O" sounds through your solar plexus as you imagine the sound drifting upward, gently, without strain or effort, touching the two points below your shoulders simultaneously. Keep your intention focused on joining the point at your solar plexus with the points just below each shoulder.

- Next, imagine an inverted triangle, the lowest corner touching the solar plexus and the other two corners located just outside your head, on either side. The left corner is the *Sefirah Binah*, understanding, and the right corner is the *Sefirah* of wisdom, *Hokhmah* (see figure 10:7). Make three "O" sounds through your solar plexus allowing the sound to drift gently upward toward

Integration

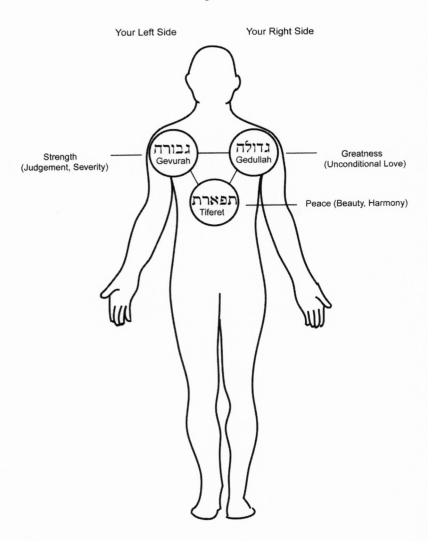

Figure 10:6

Integration

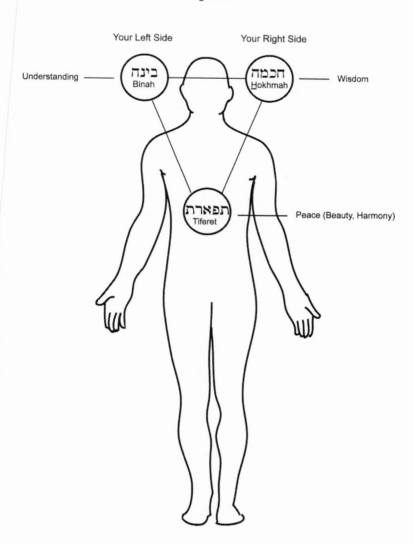

Figure 10.7

these two points outside your head simultaneous-ly. Maintain the intention of connecting your solar plexus with the two points on either side of your head.

- End this prayer by making three "O" sounds directed through the solar plexus. Keep your sounds effortless, and keep your intention focused on generating peace throughout the worlds.

Over time, you should increase the number of sounds that you make during this prayer. Eventually you should make this prayer repeating the sound of "O" a total of eighteen times. Eighteen is the number in *gematria* associated with the Hebrew word for life, *ḥai*. Make six sounds of "O" during the first part of this prayer and continue to make the "O" sound three times during the other four parts.

HEALING

· · ·

In addition to being associated with "wisdom con-sciousness," the sound of "AH," as in "rah" is associ-ated with an opening to the upper worlds.

In this Sound Prayer we chant the "AH" sound with the intention of sending healing vibrations into the world by projecting our sound through our heart center. To find the right place to project your sound, begin by making a long sigh. During the Sound Prayer we will not be sighing, but for now you will notice that when "AH" is sounded as a sigh, its vibration is experienced in the heart and upper chest. This is precisely the area we want to think of our sounds as coming through (see figure 10:8).

- Close your eyes and observe one or two minutes of silence. Concentrate on the inhalations and exhalations of your breath as you continue to relax your body. Without holding your breath or prolonging your exhalation, allow yourself to be aware of the "space" between breathing in and out.

- Visualize an inverted triangle that has its lowest point located at the solar plexus and the other two points just below the level of each shoulder. Spend a minute or two making this triangle as real as you can in your mind's eye (see figure 10:9).

- Now focus intently on the left corner of the triangle below the left shoulder. This is the one associated with the *Sefirah* that represents strength, judgement, and severity, an aspect of the Divine nature and an aspect of human nature.

- Next focus intently on the right corner of the triangle below the right shoulder. This is the location of the *Sefirah* representing greatness and

Healing Through Love

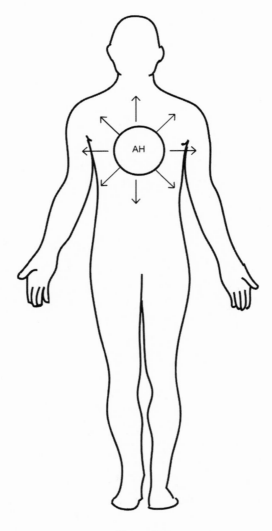

Figure 10:8

Healing Through Love

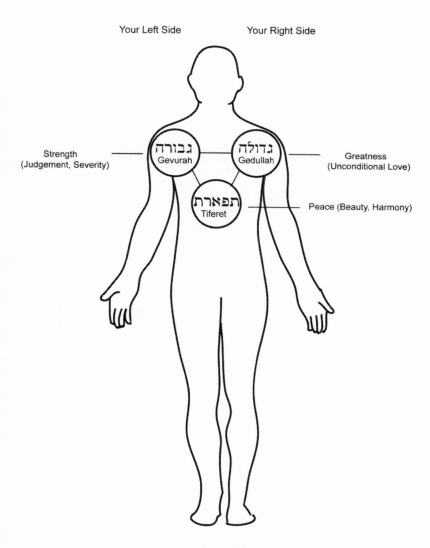

Your Left Side   Your Right Side

Strength
(Judgement, Severity) ———— גבורה Gevurah

גדולה Gedullah ———— Greatness
(Unconditional Love)

תפארת Tiferet ———— Peace (Beauty, Harmony)

Figure 10:9

unconditional love, also an aspect of the Divine nature and a part of our nature.

• Now turn your full attention to the bottom point of the triangle at the solar plexus. This is the location of the *Sefirah* representing beauty, harmony, and peace.

• Begin your prayer by very slowly making three "AH" sounds through the upper chest and heart center. Remember, this was the location to which your attention was drawn when you sighed the "AH" sound. It will help if you visualize this location on your body at the same time as you are making your sounds. As you make each sound, have it as your intention to send healing vibrations directly out into the world around you. Between each "AH" sound stay focused on this intention.

• Next, make three "AH" sounds through your heart center with the intention of sending healing to yourself, in appreciation of your struggles, your efforts, and your yearnings. If there is a specific area of your body that is troubling you, you can focus on that area.

• Next, make three "AH" sounds with the intention of sending healing to someone in your life that is giving you trouble or pain. You may notice that with this intention in mind your "AH" sound will have a different tone. This is not unusual and will not detract from the power of the prayer.

- Conclude this prayer by making three "AH" sounds through your heart center. Your intention should be to send healing toward someone you care deeply about. If possible, focus on their specific physical, emotional or spiritual needs.

Over time, you should increase the number of sounds that you make during each of the four parts of this prayer. Eventually you should make this prayer using thirty-six sounds of "AH," making nine sounds during each part. It is said that at any given time there are thirty-six righteous human beings that inhabit the world. The goodness of these beings counterbalances the forces of iniquity and evil, thus allowing for the continuation of the world. These individuals are unknown to us, yet their presence keeps the world from being overwhelmed by the forces of darkness. By using thirty-six sounds, we invoke their presence, and ask for healing through their righteousness.

ALIGNMENT

. . .

During this Sound Prayer we focus on the non-Sefirah *Sefirah*, *Daat*. Located at the throat, *Daat* has no specific vocal sound of its own, since it is related to all the sounds we make with the voice.

The two vocal sounds we use in this prayer come from two different *Sefirot*. The first is the sound of "ay" as in "say." The sound of "ay," is traditionally associated with the *Sefirah* of Understanding, *Binah*. We "borrow" the sound from *Binah* since *Binah* resides in the world of *Beriah*, or Creation, the place where the prophet Isaiah saw God's Throne. Our ultimate goal in this practice is to reach the Throne of God, so that we can be received and embraced.

Through this prayer we create channels between our heart, body, and mind by consecrating our entire being to our sacred path. Our heart and mind join through the sound of *Binah*, while our physical body is dedicated to its higher purpose through the sound of *Yesod* (see figure 10:10).

- Close your eyes and observe one or two minutes of silence. Concentrate on the inhalations and exhalations of your breath as you relax your body. Without holding your breath or prolonging your exhalation, allow yourself to be aware of the "space" between breathing in and out.

- Keeping your eyes closed, visualize your heart center, the place from which your yearning extends. Focus on this place on your body for a short time.

Aligning with the Upper Worlds

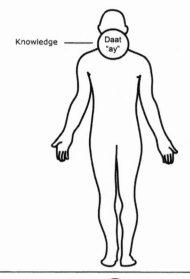

Knowledge ———— Daat "ay"

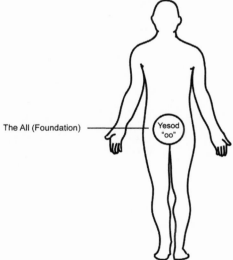

The All (Foundation) ———— Yesod "oo"

Figure 10:10

- Make three "ay" sounds as in "say," projecting the sound through the throat and *Daat,* while drawing support from your heart. Your intention should be to reach upward as high as you possibly can with all the yearning you can bring to bear. Before continuing, remain silent for as long as you feel the need.

- Then in order to ground yourself, conclude your prayer with three low sounds of "oo" as in "too." Project your sounds through your genital area, the place of *Yesod,* while imagining that the sounds you are making are reaching all the way up to your throat and then down again to your genital area. This may not be easy at first, but with practice you will find that the circular path of your sounds becomes easier and easier to visualize and gives you great support.

Over time you may wish to increase the number of sounds you make in this prayer. It is recommended that you do so by increasing the number of "oo" sounds to a maximum of six, while keeping the number of "ay" sounds limited to three. This prayer should be made no more than twice a day, once in the morning and once in the evening.

THE SOUND OF THE FLAME

The Great Octave
plucked with the Breath of Life,
reverberates the spheres.
Vibrations—
the length
and breadth
of manifested creation.

Enveloping
the fruits,
Oscillations
return to the Source,
nurturing the Emanator.

The Flame listens and warms.

Appendices

TRANSLITERATION TABLE

Alphabet		Num. Value	Transliteration
א	Aleph	1	A
בּ,ב	Bet, Vet	2	B, V
ג	Gimel	3	G
ד	Dalet	4	D
ה	Heh	5	H
ו	Vav	6	V (also O and U)
ז	Zayin	7	Z
ח	Het	8	H
ט	Tet	9	T
י	Yud	10	Y, I
כ,כּ	Kaf, Khaf	20	K, KH
ל	Lamed	30	L
מ	Mem	40	M
נ	Nun	50	N
ס	Sameh	60	S
ע	Ayin	70	silent or A
פּ,פ	Pay, Phay	80	P, PH or F
צ	Tzadee	90	Tz
ק	Kuf	100	K
ר	Resh	200	R
שׁ,שׂ	Shin, Sin	300	Sh, SS
ת	Tav	400	T

Final Letters (when the letter appears at the end of a word)

ך	Khaf	500	KH
ם	Mem	600	M
ן	Nun	700	N
ף	Phay	800	Ph or F
ץ	Tzadee	900	Tz

GLOSSARY OF TERMS

Note: Both the <u>H</u> (underlined) and the KH in the English transliterations are pronounced as a guttural "ch." While they are pronounced the same, they actually represent two different letters within the Hebrew alphabet, *<u>H</u>et* (ח) and *Khaf* (כ). (see the Transliteration Table). They should not be confused with the sound of H or the sound of K.

Terms	Pronunciation	Meaning
Adam Kadmon	Ah-**dahm** Kahd-**mone**	Primordial, Archetypal Man
Adonai	Ah-doh-**nai**	God Name
A<u>h</u>lama	A<u>h</u>-la-**mah**	Beautiful Gem (Amethyst)
Aleph	**Ah**-leph (A)	A (Letter of the Alphabet)
Bahir	Bah-**here**	Illumination (*Kabbalah* Text)
Bereshit	Bre-**sheet**	In the Beginning
Bet	**Bait** (B)	B (Alphabet)
Binah	Bee-**naw**	Understanding (A *Sefirah*)
Brakhah	Bra-**khah**	Blessing
Brekhah	Brey-**khah**	Pool of Water
Dai	**Die**	Enough
Dvekut	Dve-**koot**	Devotion, Cleaving to God
Derekh Hashem	De-rekh Ha-**shem**	Path of God (by Luzzatto)
Daat	**Dah**-aht	Knowing
Din	**Deen**	Judgement
Ein Sof	**Ain Sofe**	The Endless One
Elohim	*E-lo-**heem**	God Name
	*(when not praying say El-o-**keem**)	
El-Shaddai	**Elle** Sha-**die**	God Name
Emet	Eh-**met**	Truth
Etz <u>H</u>aim	Etz <u>H</u>a-**yim**	Tree of Life
Gedullah	Gedoo-**lah**	Greatness (A *Sefirah*)
Gematria	Gee-**mah**-treeah	Numerology

Terms	Pronunciation	Meaning
Gevurah	Gevoo-**rah**	Strength, Might (A *Sefirah*)
Haim	Ha-**yim**	Life
Hakbalah	Hak-bah-**lah**	Parallels
Halom	Ha-**lome**	Dream
Hashem	Hah-**shem**	"The Name," Word for God
Hashmal	Hash-**mal**	Speech/Silence, Rapidity/Pause
Hay	**Hay** (H)	H (Letter of Alphabet)
Hayah	Hah-**yah**	Soul Essence, Also the type of Angel (Literally: Living)
Hayot	Hah-**yote**	Angels (A Class of Angels)
Hesed	He-**sed**	Grace
Het	**Het**	Error, Sin
Hirik	Hee-**reek**	Vowel Point
Hod	**Hoed**	Splendor (*Sefirah* through which we manifest vision)
Hoddah	Ho-**dah**	He Acknowledged
Hokhmah	Hokh-**mah**	Wisdom (A *Sefirah*)
Holam	Ho-**lam**	Vowel Point
Holayim	Ho-lah-**yim**	Diseases
Ilat Hailot	E-**lot** Ha-ee-**lote**	Cause of Causes
Kabbalah	Kah-bah-**lah**	Receiving, Reception
Kamatz	Kah-**matz**	Vowel Point
Kavanah	Kah-vah-**nah**	Intention
Kelipot	Klee-**pote**	Shells, Powers of Evil
Karet	**Ka**-ret	Cut off
Kesher	Ke-**sher**	Tie
Keter	**Ke**-ter	Crown (A *Sefirah*)
Kitur	Kee-**tour**	Surround
Koah mah	Ko-ah **Mah**	Power of What
Kubutz	Koo-**boots**	Vowel Sound
Kivun	Key-**voon**	Direction
Kol	**Kol**	Voice, Sound
Kol Dmamah	**Kol** Dmah-**mah**	Sound of Silence
Lamed	Lah-**med**	L (letter of Alphabet)
Lev	**Lev**	Heart
Likkutei Amarim-Tanya	Lik-koo-**tei** Ama-**reem**, **Tan**-ya	Gathering of Teachings (by Rabbi Zalman)

Terms	Pronunciation	Meaning
Maggid	Mah-**geed**	"One who tells" or Answering Angel
Maggidim	Mah-gee-**deem**	Plural of Maggid
Malakh	Mal-**akh**	Angel
Malakhim	Mal-ah-**kheem**	Angels
Malkhut	Mal-**khoot**	Kingdom (A *Sefirah*)
Mem	**Mem**	M (Letter of the Alphabet)
Merkavah	Mer-ka-**vah**	Chariot, Assembly
Nekud	Nee-**kud**	System of Vowel Points
Nekudot	Ne-ku-**dote**	Vowel Points
Nefesh	Ne-**fesh**	Vital Animal Soul
Neshamah	Nshah-**mah**	Higher Soul
Neshimah	Nshi-**mah**	Breath
Netzah	Ne-**tzah**	Eternity, Victory (*Sefirah* where vision is located)
Nishmat Haim	Neesh-**mat** Ha-**yim**	Breath of Life
Olam haAssiyah	Oh-**lam** ha-Ah-see-**yah**	The World of the Concrete
Olam haAtzilut	Oh-**lam** ha-Ah-tzee-**lute**	The World of Emanation
Olam haBeriah	Oh-**lam** ha-Bree-**ah**	The World of Creation
Olam haYetzirah	Oh-**lam** ha-Yetzee-**rah**	The World of Formation
Ophanim	Oh-phah-**neem**	Wheels, Angels
Patah	Pah-**tah**	Vowel Sound
Pithey	Peet-**hey**	Openings
Reishit	Ray-**sheet**	Beginning
Ruah	**Ru**-ah	Spirit, Wind, Breath
Sefer Yetzirah	Se-fer Yetzee-**rah**	Book of Formation
Sefer haZohar	Se-fer Ha-**Zo**-har	The Book of Splendor
Sefirah	Sfee-**rah**	Emanation of the Tree of Life (Literally: Counting)
Sefirot	Sfee-**rote**	Plural of *Sefirah*
Segol	Se-**gole**	Vowel sound
Segullah	Sgoo-**lah**	Treasury, Unique Attribute
Sha'ar ha-Nikud	**Sha**-ar ha-Nee-**kud**	The Gate of the Vowel Points (by Gikatila)
Sha'are Orah	Sha-ah-**rey** O-**rah**	Gates of Light (by Gikatila)
Shad	**Shadd**	Breast
Shaddai	Sha-**die**	My Breasts

Terms	Pronunciation	Meaning
Shed	**Shed**	Demon
Shekhinah	Shkhee-**nah**	Indwelling Female Aspect of God
Shevirah	Shvee-**rah**	Shattering of the Vessels
Shir Hashirim	**Sheer** Ha-shee-**reem**	Song of Songs
Shofar	Sho-**far**	Ram's Horn
Shulamit(e)	Shu-la-**meet**	A Woman from the Clan of the Shulamites, The Beloved of the Song of Songs
Shuruk	Shoo-**rook**	Vowel Sound
Shva	Shva	Vowel Sound
Siddur	See-**doore**	Jewish Prayer Book
Talmud	Tal-**mood**	Commentaries on *Torah* and *Mishnah*
Tanakh	Ta-**nakh**	Holy Scripture
Tav	**Tav**	T, Letter of the Alphabet
Tiferet	Teef-**eh**-ret	Beauty, Glory (A *Sefirah*)
Tikkun Olam	Tee-**koon** Oh-**lam**	Repair of the World
Tikkuney Zohar	Teek-koo-**ney Zo**-har	Amendments to the *Zohar* (Part of the *Zohar* Text)
Torah	To-**rah**	Five Books of Moses
Tzaddik	Tza-**deek**	Righteous Person
Tzerey	Tze-**rey**	Vowel Point
Tzimtzum	Tzeem-**tzoom**	Contraction
Tzinnor	Tzee-**nor**	Channel
Tzinnorot	Tzee-no-**rote**	Channels
Vav	**Vawv**	Hook, Letter of the Alphabet
Yadah	Yah-**dah**	He Knew
Yehidah	Yehee-**dah**	Oneness, Unit
Yeshivah	Yeshee-**vah**	School of *Torah* Study
Yesod	Ye-**sode**	Foundation/The All (A *Sefirah*)
Yetzer	Ye-**tzer**	Impulse
Yetzer haRah	Ye-tzer Ha-**rah**	Force of Evil
Yetzer haTov	Ye-tzer Ha-**tov**	Force of Good
YHVH	Unpronounceable	Holy Name of God
Yud	**Yood**	Letter of the Alphabet/Symbol for Name of God
Zohar	**Zo**-har	Splendor, *Kabbalah* Text

NOTES

Chapter One: The Path of *Kabbalah*

1. *Genesis* 3:22–24.
2. *NB*: There is some disagreement among scholars as to the authorship and the exact dates of origin of these *Kabbalah* texts.
3. See for example Gershom Scholem, *Sabbatai Sevi, The Mystical Messiah* (Princeton: Princeton University Press, 1973).
4. *Exodus* 3:6.
5. See for example the *Zohar* (London: Soncino Press, 1984), 1:15A–15B; *Tikkuney haZohar* (Jerusalem: Yarid Hasfarim, n.d.), Tikkun 70, p. 679; *Torat Hakana Sefer haBahir* (Jerusalem: Nezer Schraga, 1990), # 40–44, pp. 19–21; and Rabbi Joseph Gikatila, *Sha'ar haNekud* (Jerusalem: Yarid Hasfarim, 1994).
6. Rabbi Joseph Gikatila, *Sha'ar haNekud* (Jerusalem: Yarid Hasfarim, 1994), p. 3.
7. *1 Kings* 3:9.

Chapter Two: The Curtain of Souls

1. *Sefer Yetzirah* (Jerusalem: Yeshivot Kol Yehuda, 1990), p. 55.
2. *Job* 33:15–16.
3. *Zohar* (London: Soncino Press, 1984), 2:183A.
4. *Genesis* 2:7.
5. *Deuteronomy* 4:4.
6. Moses Haim Luzzatto, *Derekh Hashem* (Jerusalem: Feldheim, 1966), p. 90.

Chapter Three: Cultivating the Garden

1. Rabbi Schneur Zalman, *Likkutei Amarim-Tanya* (Brooklyn: Kehot Publication Society, 1984), p. 281.
2. *Ibid.*, p. 81.
3. *Ecclesiastes* 7:20.
4. *Exodus* 20:3.

Chapter Four: Angels

1. *Tikkuney haZohar* (Jerusalem: Yarid Hasfarim, n.d.), Introduction.
2. *Zohar* (London: Soncino Press, 1984), 1:53B.
3. *Ibid.,* 2:165B.
4. *Isaiah* 6:5.
5. *Isaiah* 6:7.
6. Rabbi Joseph Gikatila, *Sha'are Orah* (Jerusalem: Yarid Hasfarim, 1994), Sha'ar Aleph, p. 6.

Chapter Five: The Names of God

1. *Exodus* 6:2–3.
2. Rabbi Schneur Zalman, *Likkutei Amarim-Tanya* (Brooklyn: Kehot Publication Society, 1984), p. 90.
3. *Deuteronomy* 1:17.
4. The prohibition against pronouncing *YHVH* is thought to have begun during the Babylonian exile.
5. Rabbi Joseph Gikatila, *Sha'are Orah* (Jerusalem: Yarid Hasfarim, 1994), Sha'ar Aleph, p. 3.
6. *Genesis* 2:4.

Chapter Six: The Tree of Life

1. *Zohar* (London: Soncino Press, 1984), 1:15a, 16b.
2. *Exodus* 31:3.
3. *1 Chronicles* 29:11.
4. *Exodus* 3:14.
5. *Ezekiel* 1:14, *Sefer Yetzirah* (Jerusalem:Yeshivot Kol Yehuda, 1990), p. 57.
6. *Mikhah* 7:20.
7. *Genesis* 18:1–8.
8. *Genesis* 31:53.
9. Rabbi Nehuniah ben Hakana, *Torat Hakana, Sefer haBahir* (Jerusalem: Nezer Schraga), #135, p. 59.
10. *Ibid.,* #75, p. 35.
11. *Genesis* 25:27.
12. *Mikhah* 7:20.
13. *Exodus* 4:15–16.
14. *Proverbs* 10:25.

15. *Sefer Yetzirah* (Yeshivot Kol Yehuda, 1990), p. 60.
16. *Zohar* (London: Soncino Press, 1984), 2:172A.
17. *Exodus* 32:8.
18. *Exodus* 31:3.
19. *Genesis* 4:1.

Chapter Eight: Sound Prayer

1. *Exodus* 25:2, 8.
2. *Deuteronomy* 6:5.
3. *Sefer Yetzirah* (Jerusalem: Yeshivot Kol Yehuda, 1990), p. 55.
4. *Zohar* (London: Soncino Press, 1984), 1:15A–15B.
5. *Sefer Yetzirah*, p. 59.
6. *Genesis* 1:3.
7. *Genesis* 1: 1–2.
8. *Exodus* 20:15.
9. *Zohar* 1:15B.
10. *Genesis* 2:7.
11. *1 Kings* 19:12.
12. *Ezekiel* 1:4.
13. *Isaiah* 42:14.
14. Moses Maimonides, *Guide for the Perplexed* (London: Pardes Publishing House, 1904), 3:4, p. 260.
15. *Genesis* 1:6–8.
16. *Sha'are Orah,* Sha'ar Aleph, (Jerusalem: Yarid Hasfarim, 1994), p. 6.
17. *Sefer haZohar*, (Jerusalem: Yarid Hasfarim, n.d.), pp. 125–126.
18. *Zohar* (London: Soncino Press, 1984), 2:167B–168A.

Chapter Nine: The Sacred Sounds of the *Sefirot*

1. *Zohar* (London: Soncino Press, 1984), 1:15B.
2. Rabbi Nehuniah ben Hakana, *Torat Hakana, Sefer haBahir* (Jerusalem: Nezer Schraga, n.d.), #115, p. 53.
3. *Ibid.,* #116, p. 53.
4. *Ezekiel* 1:20.
5. *Tikkuney haZohar* (Jerusalem: Yarid Hasfarim, n.d.), Tikkun 70.
6. Psalm 24:7.
7. *Isaiah* 6:1.
8. *Tikkuney haZohar* (Jerusalem: Yarid Hasfarim, n.d.), Tikkun 21. The *segol* is also related to the *segolta,* one of the cantillation

marks used when chanting Holy Scripture. The cantillation marks indicate melody and emphasis.

9. *Torat Hakana, Sefer haBahir* (Jerusalem: Nezer Schraga, n.d.), #89, p. 40.

10. Depending on its placement in a word, the *shva* can also be silent.

11. *Job* 1:15.

12. Rabbi Joseph Gikatila, *Sha'ar ha Nekud* (Jerusalem: Yarid Hasfarim, 1994), p. 19.

13. *Ibid.*, p. 116.

14. Rabbi Nehuniah ben Hakana, *Torat Hakana, Sefer haBahir* (Jerusalem: Nezer Schraga, 1990), #40, p. 19.

15. *Ibid.*, #43, p. 23.

16. *Ezekiel* 1:22.

17. *Sefer haZohar* (Jerusalem: Yarid Hasfarim, n.d.), p. 160.

18. Although the sounds for *Hod* and *Yesod* are described as similar, when they are used in Sound Prayer, the intention that accompanies each of them are different. As a result, the vibration of the two sounds will differ.

19. *Sha'ar haNekud*, (Jerusalem: Yarid Hasfarim, 1994), pp. 14–15.

20. *Sefer Yetzirah* (Jerusalem: Yeshivot Kol Yehuda, 1990), p. 55.

Chapter Ten: Sound Prayer Instruction

1. *Esther* 4:2.

BIBLIOGRAPHY

Ben Hakana, Rabbi Nehuniah. *Torat Hakana, Sefer haBahir*. Jerusalem: Nezer Schraga, 1997.

Elson, Shulamit. *Brooklyn Bodhisattvas, A Book of Visions and Kabballistic Poetry*. High Falls: SoulSongs Publishing, 1999.

Gikatila, Rabbi Joseph. *Sha'are Orah*. Jerusalem: Yarid Hasfarim, 1994.

_____. *Sha'ar haNekud*. Jerusalem: Yarid Hasfarim, 1994.

Luzzatto, Moses Haim. *Derekh Hashem*. Jerusalem: Feldheim, 1966.

Maimonides, Moses. *The Guide for the Perplexed*. London: Pardes Publishing House, 1904. Translated from the Arabic by Michael Friedlander, Ph.D.

Mishnah, Seder Nizikin, Second Edition Vol. 2. Jerusalem: Mishnayot Kehati, 1997.

Scholem, Gershom. *Sabbatai Sevi, The Mystical Messiah*. Princeton, New Jersey: Princeton University Press, 1973. Translated from the Hebrew by Dr. R.J. Zwi Werblowsky.

Sefer haZohar. Jerusalem: Yarid Hasfarim, n.d. Translated into Hebrew from Aramaic and Hebrew text by Rabbi Shlomo Cohen.

Sefer Yetzirah. Jerusalem: Yeshivat Kol Yehuda, 1990.

Tanakh

Tikkuney haZohar. Jerusalem: Yarid Hasfarim, n.d. Translated into Hebrew from the Aramaic and Hebrew by Rabbi Shlomo Cohen.

Zalman, Rabbi Schneur. *Likkutei Amarim-Tanya*. Brooklyn: Kehot Publication Society, 1984. Translated into English by Dr. Nissan Mindel.

Zohar. London: Soncino Press, 1984. 6 Volumes. Translated into English by Harry Sperling, Maurice Simon, and Dr. Paul Levertoff.